Meditation
MADE EASY

MORE THAN 50 EXERCISES FOR PEACE, RELAXATION, & MINDFULNESS

PRESTON BENTLEY

Adams Media
New York London Toronto Sydney New Delhi

Adams Media
An Imprint of Simon & Schuster, Inc.
57 Littlefield Street
Avon, Massachusetts 02322

For information about special discounts for bulk purchases, please contact Simon & Schuster Special Sales at 1-866-506-1949 or business@simonandschuster.com.

The Simon & Schuster Speakers Bureau can bring authors to your live event. For more information or to book an event contact the Simon & Schuster Speakers Bureau at 1-866-248-3049 or visit our website at www.simonspeakers.com.

Manufactured in the United States of America

10 9 8 7 6 5

Library of Congress Cataloging-in-Publication Data has been applied for.

ISBN 978-1-4405-8432-9
ISBN 978-1-4405-8433-6 (ebook)

Contents

Introduction

Meditation is supposed to quiet you, to focus your mind on just one thing. Yet these days, who has the time for that?

Sometimes, people think of meditation as sitting in painful positions for hours, just waiting for something to happen. Though sitting still is one way to meditate, there are many other options, too. No matter what you are doing or what is going on in your life, you can *choose* to do it with your full presence, thereby performing it mindfully. That's meditation! You can mindfully drink your tea, take a shower, or cook dinner, and all it takes is focus and intention, doing what you do moment by moment, breath by breath. Anything you do mindfully becomes a meditation if you do it with calm and attention. Stretching, executing a yoga pose, and even taking a walk all can be meditations.

As you practice meditation, you will discover the keys that open the door to your potential as a human being. In this place, you'll find ways of meeting challenges and coping with problems. You'll also find new ways to engage your life with experience that teaches, heals, and enhances everything around you. It will take some work, but it is a labor of love you deserve.

If discovering greater meaning and purpose in life isn't reason enough to begin a meditation practice, the physical benefits should be. Over the past few decades, evidence has been mounting that suggests that meditation helps to reduce the harmful effects of stressful lifestyles.

Want to have more energy? Reduce the risk of a heart attack? Control depression and anxiety? Often, our first response to such problems is to reach for a pill bottle, but perhaps more ancient ways of combating them should be employed alongside modern Western medicine. Perhaps people living thousands of years ago had some wisdom about life that we have lost in our fast-paced, technology-driven societies. And yet, at the same time, our technology and science help us to understand ancient practices better, to find explanations for how and why they work.

The practice of meditation should be at the core of your life. It's the basic tool that allows every act to have meaning and richness. Meditation doesn't have to be a separate, "special" event that takes you away from your responsibilities or leisure. It can be an ongoing process that is part of everything that you do.

If meditation is an idea you want to explore, what is the best way to go about it? And if you already occasionally meditate, how can you develop and grow with it?

This book offers a simple, approachable introduction to meditation, with a wide variety of exercises you can do at any time of day, no matter where you are. The meditations vary in length and are adaptable and interchangeable, according to your needs. You'll find breathing exercises that can help you quickly calm down in stressful situations, short and long meditations designed to help you slow down and experience what is happening within you and outside of you, prayers and mantras that can help you stay present in the moment and state your intentions for the day, and yoga poses that help you connect what's happening in your mind with what's happening in your body.

Some of these exercises are perfect for when you first wake up in the morning, before you've even gotten out of bed. Others might be just right for a break at work. You might choose to do a morning meditation practice, or perhaps you'll find you prefer to meditate before getting ready for bed at night. Sometimes you might enjoy the silence, and other times you might choose to play calming music during your practice. When, where, why, and how you meditate is entirely up to you.

No matter how or why you begin a meditation practice, there is no better time to start than right now. Being in the present is what it's all about, and if you enter into the experience with an open heart and mind you will begin to see the benefits in all areas of your life. Get ready to tap into the everyday miracle of meditation by simply setting aside a few minutes each day to foster peace and tranquility.

PART I

Meditation Basics

What Is Meditation?

You've no doubt heard that meditation can help remedy the ills of modern living: stress, anxiety, depression, and poor health. It is also praised for its healing benefits and positive influence on personal well-being and relationships. But what, exactly, is meditation? In a nutshell, meditation is the stilling of all your conscious faculties in order to be present in the moment. This may be a foreign concept to you, or something you think only "enlightened" people do. You may also think it requires a lot of time and involves a learning curve. The truth? Meditation is a simple practice—something anyone can do, anywhere, anytime.

For the purposes of this book, meditation includes anything from simple breathing exercises, to reciting (or merely thinking of) prayers or mantras, to guided imagery, to yoga poses. It can be as simple and as pleasurable as gazing out a window and watching a bird at the feeder. Some meditations last a matter of seconds, while others can last as long as twenty minutes or more. With meditation, there is no right or wrong. When, where, how, and why are all up to you.

Misconceptions about Meditation

When considering meditation, you might first think of a Buddhist monk wearing a robe, sitting cross-legged on a mountaintop, far from the realities of everyday life. With eyes closed, perfect posture, and an immobile expression, the meditator appears to be in another world, above and beyond the demands that the rest of us are dealing with on a daily basis. This image seems neither possible to emulate nor worthwhile as a goal. While that is one way to meditate, it's certainly not the *only* way.

You can meditate in any clothes you want, anywhere that's convenient for you. Meditation requires no special separation from daily life. You do not have to give up your creature comforts in order to embrace meditation. In fact, meditation allows you to appreciate and understand their presence in your life.

In addition, although perfect posture and immobility are skills that you can learn through meditation, they are not the purpose of the practice. Physical conditioning does play a fundamental role in meditation, but you don't have to stand on your head or contort your body to achieve balance or harmony. Natural postures, movements, and breathing are all that you need to start a meditation practice. You may quickly learn, however, that what you have been doing for some time is not natural after all. For example, when you sit in a chair without thinking about it, you might actually be hunched over or slouching. Paying close attention to your body is one part of learning to meditate.

You Might Already Be Meditating Without Knowing It!

Did you know that you often enter a meditative state under everyday circumstances without knowing it? You might actually already be achieving some self-awareness while performing simple, methodical tasks that free your mind from concentrated thought. Such tasks often disengage feelings which can distract your attention. For example:

- **Engaging in challenging sports:** Athletes frequently speak of the mental freedom they attain when their bodies are completely involved in meeting a challenge, such as running a long distance or climbing a steep incline.
- **Nursing a baby:** Some mothers find serenity while breastfeeding, which enhances the bonding process with the infant and also brings a unique connection to life itself.
- **Performing strenuous physical work:** The rigor of a physical task, such as carrying heavy loads with great care, can bring uncommon mind-body awareness.

- **Washing dishes:** Performing such a familiar task (accompanied by the soothing sounds of water) often frees the mind to become aware of itself.

In these instances it is the realization—without thought or feeling—that you are participating in the moment that brings you into the state of meditation.

The Language of Meditation

While certain words have established meanings, in the context of meditation practice they can take on other meanings as well. For example:

- **Awareness:** Using your physical senses to enhance your perception of the present; involves the faculties of hearing, seeing, body sensation, and breath.
- **Contemplation:** Using all your faculties (the senses of sight, sound, touch, smell, and taste) and your conscious attention to learn as much as possible about one idea or image; allows all of your senses to become consciously involved in an experience.
- **Focus:** Training yourself to place attention on a single idea or image—and to bring your attention back when you become distracted.
- **Visualization:** Bringing to mind an object or scene that assists in fulfilling a specific purpose.

The Benefits of Meditation

When you first begin to meditate, you may wonder what's so great about sitting quietly and watching your breath. You will feel useless and restless, like you are wasting time. At first, you will feel an overwhelming urge to go back to frantic activity, but this will pass.

Mental Benefits

After sitting for a meditation session or two, you will already begin to feel better, more content, and more rested. Once you establish a regular pattern of meditation, you will feel happier and less anxious. The world itself will seem more vibrant, like you have switched from black-and-white to color. In terms of the performance of your mind, your memory and concentration will improve. You will begin to see larger connections and patterns in your life that you never noticed before. You will see how small events fit into the grand scheme of things. This will remove some of the tedium and weariness of life. It's like hitting the refresh button on your own existence.

After still more practice, the nagging problems of your life will seem less severe and less important. Your mood will improve. Stress and anxiety will lessen. You will work fluidly and intuitively rather than obsessing over small details.

Physical Benefits

More tangibly, meditation helps you decrease your heart rate, blood pressure, and cholesterol levels. Research conducted at the Cedars-Sinai Medical Center in Los Angeles found that individuals with coronary heart disease who practiced meditation experienced lower blood pressure and improved blood glucose and insulin levels. Over a lifetime, meditation will reduce your risk of heart disease, diabetes, and stroke.

Overall Well-Being

Meditation will also make you more likely to make other positive lifestyle changes, like eating well and exercising. The benefits of meditation grow exponentially as you start taking charge of your life and well-being.

Meditation and Your "Mind"

Common sense says that the brain commands and controls the rest of the body, like a puppet master controls the strings of a puppet, or a drill sergeant barks orders at cadets. The command-and-control idea of the brain has a certain amount of truth to it, but the reality is actually much more cooperative than these images suggest. Your "mind," which actually includes more than just your brain, describes the ways that the body's many systems interact with your brain and the environment to produce experiences.

How Your Mind and Body Interact

Think of your "mind" as a triangle consisting of the brain, the body, and the surrounding environment. Each of the three points in this system has a complex structure of its own. For example, the brain has numerous processing centers. Neural elements extend downward into the heart and lungs, and, through the spinal column, reach every part of the body. Then, there are the other processes taking place in the body: respiration, circulation, and digestion, for example, as well as endocrine and renal functions. The organs, systems, and cells of the body execute trillions of functions every second, and the wondrous part of it all is that the vast majority happens without any conscious effort on your part.

Yet, the thoughts that pass through your head and the emotions associated with those thoughts *do* matter and can affect all of these unseen processes to a profound degree. The quality of the environment certainly also affects consciousness and health. For example, depriving a person of a suitable and stimulating environment will impair social and cognitive development, just as providing a very rich environment will help in producing a healthy intellectual and emotional life.

Harmonizing Your Mind and Body

Some factors that influence the triangle lie outside of your control. You can't alter your DNA, for example (at least not yet), and we have to put up with a certain amount of toxicity and stress as part of our modern, industrialized consumer lifestyles. You may even have persistent (though not inevitable) features of your personality that can be very difficult to overcome. Anger, depression, and anxiety have become invisible plagues in society, affecting almost every aspect of our common life. Fortunately, meditation and deep, slow breathing can balance the triangle of body, brain, and environment, returning your experience of the world to a more neutral, peaceful state.

The Importance of Your Breathing

You may wonder why breathing is a central component in meditation and why it is emphasized so much. After all, breathing is a natural, autonomic function of your body. Even so, you might not be maximizing your oxygen intake with each breath.

The Dangers of Ineffective Breathing

Have you ever listened to your breathing? Or observed your rhythm of inhaling and exhaling? Try it. You might find that you breathe in short breaths that do not completely fill your lungs. Once you notice, you can start to consciously take deeper breaths. Though it may sound counter-intuitive, deep, slow breathing actually causes the cells in the body to consume less oxygen, which reduces the amount of stress on the body. This kind of breathing has the same effect as small, regular meals have on your calorie intake. If you starve yourself during a busy day, the usual outcome is an evening binge. A skipped lunch may become a late-afternoon break for candy and soda. When the body experiences gaps in regular eating, it compensates by lowering metabolism to conserve energy. In the same way, deep, slow breathing produces increased oxygenation, which means that the heart doesn't have to work as hard to supply the body with oxygen, which leads to lowered blood pressure and a lower heart rate. The effect on your heart is similar to the effect of aerobic exercise.

Breathing deeply is like saying to the circulatory system, "Look, everything is okay. Just relax." Some yogis (practitioners of yoga) believe that short breaths lead to a short lifespan, while long breaths lead to a long lifespan. While it would be difficult to quantify the effects of deep breathing over a lifetime of practice, evidence suggests that deliberate, regular practice will alleviate symptoms of high blood pressure and cardiovascular disease.

Breathing Meets Visualization

Beyond the deep-breathing aspect of meditation, the thinking process also plays an important role. You may have noticed how a single negative thought leads to a chain of other negative thoughts. You stub your toe getting out of bed and, after some other choice phrases, say to yourself, "This just isn't my day." The negative aspects of the morning are then multiplied: the commute seems more annoying than usual, as does the stream of e-mails in your inbox. By mid-morning you feel like screaming and you have a headache, and it only gets worse from there.

In this case, your brain and the body have entered into a negative feedback loop. Negative thoughts induce a negative emotional state, which has a physiological response. Emotional turmoil triggers the fight-or-flight response, and after the rush subsides, you are left feeling wasted, in a state that feels much like a hangover. You might have feelings of sadness and inadequacy, along with physical pain and a general sense of lethargy. A coffee break helps, but it doesn't really get rid of the problem, and the cycle begins all over again.

Meditation can help with the process of negotiating life's woes, not by just telling yourself that everything is peachy keen, but by pausing the downward cycle of negative thoughts and feelings. The purpose of visualization and mantra practice is to put a placeholder before consciousness which interrupts the flow of oppressive, dark thoughts and emotions. Rather than fighting the negative thoughts and emotions, this practice accepts and *replaces* negative thoughts and emotions. The body will begin to believe in the visualization and will stop responding as though the world were falling apart. Positive visualizations achieve some of the same effects as deep, slow breathing.

When combined, these two techniques can be a powerful antidote to stress-induced disorders.

The Basics of Breath Control

Your body's natural response to stress causes shallow breathing and a rapid heart rate, which prepares your body to encounter a physical threat. Stress also triggers an emotional response that begins in panic or anxiety and can lead to sadness and depression. The good news is that controlling your breath with meditation interferes with this downward spiral and reverses it. How can it do that? The answer is based in the physiology of the body. A complex network of nerves runs from the top of your head to the tips of your toes. This neural system sends signals at lightning pace throughout your body. You'll feel a change in one part of your body throughout your whole body. Giving someone a foot massage doesn't just relax their feet; it sends pleasurable relaxation throughout their entire body.

Conscious Breathing

In the same way, a network connects your brain, heart, and lungs. The interplay between these three organs prepares your body for any situation that it might encounter. Since it's a self-regulating system, most of the time you don't need to think about breathing. But you can, of course, take conscious control of your breathing whenever you like. This is where nature has given you a tool to take control of negative thoughts and emotions. A perceived threat will speed up the heart and lungs in order to prepare the body for an emergency situation. When you instead begin breathing deeply, you manually intervene in the stress response. The interplay between brain and lungs is a two-way street. When you breathe deeply, you send an "all is well" signal to the brain that lets it know that it should slow the heart rate. You also send plenty of oxygen to the lungs. This sends a signal to the heart that it can afford to slow down.

That's how meditation can lower your heart rate and your blood pressure: More available oxygen means that the heart-lung-brain system can do less work to accomplish the same results.

Everyday Breath Control

Your body's stress response is triggered subconsciously; your brain can't tell the difference between a real threat and a fake one. Remembering that big report due Monday morning can lead to panic just as facing a bear at a campsite would. Multitasking also induces stress, as the brain struggles to switch back and forth between competing tasks.

Although you probably can't avoid stressful situations entirely, you *can* learn to control how your brain responds to them. By breathing more deeply and slowly when you start to feel stressed, you keep your system on an even keel and reduce the customary rush of stress hormones. This approach is simple, but it may not come easy to you. You may have learned to thrive on the adrenaline rush that comes from always burning the candle at both ends. You may be a stress-hormone junkie who needs that extra kick to avoid procrastination and get things done.

Once you start practicing breath control, you won't feel that breathless, panicked sensation. You won't feel the butterflies in your stomach or the pounding in your chest. Instead, you will feel something different and (at first) strange: a calm, steady feeling. The same things that used to provoke your ire no longer will. What might have ranked an 8 or 9 on a stress scale of 1–10 will now rank a 3 or 4. The result? You'll have a tremendous reserve of surplus energy that you can channel into finding creative solutions to the problem that caused you stress in the first place.

Breath Control, Step by Step

Deep, slow breathing begins to work almost immediately, but it is something you'll get better at the more you practice. Try this progression:

1. In the beginning, try inhaling for eight seconds, holding for four seconds, exhaling for eight seconds, and holding for four seconds.
2. For deliberate practice, start with five minutes of breath work each morning and evening and gradually increase from there. In addition, any time you feel anxious, do a few repetitions to calm yourself.
3. Build to inhaling for twelve seconds, holding for six seconds, exhaling for twelve seconds, and holding for six seconds. This will become the foundation for your meditation practice.

See how portable and manageable breath control can be? You can do it in line at the supermarket, while driving, or while sitting at your desk. To get the full effect, though, you will want to devote a few minutes each day to exclusively focusing on breathing. Feel your lungs expand and contract. Watch your breath flow in and out. Count mentally as you go. Once you have the rhythm down, you can stop counting and just concentrate on the breath. This practice has a cumulative effect: Each session builds on the previous one as you reconfigure your body's systems. Your daily start point of agitation will change as you move more deeply into the practice.

Observing Your Thoughts

Most paths of meditation recommend "watching" your own thoughts as they arise, taking the standpoint of an observer in your own head, and becoming aware of all of the words, images, and feelings that present themselves. That might sound a little difficult at first.

"Watching" your thoughts takes practice. The best way to start is to—what else?—practice your breathing.

Clearing Your Mind via Deep Breathing

Deep breaths allow you to clear your mind and give yourself an opportunity to see your thoughts. Try this exercise:

- Count from one to five as you breathe in. Don't worry about breath control for now; just breathe normally. Concentrate on just the numbers one through five.
- As soon as your mind begins to wander, start over again at one. If you think about what you might have for lunch or the next item on your agenda, start over at one. You may find yourself rarely, if ever, making it to five.
- If you do make it to five, start over again at one. Avoid the temptation to count while simultaneously thinking of other things, as this defeats the purpose of the exercise.

Notice how, at first, your mind flits from topic to topic in perpetual activity? With practice, you'll be able to stop that cycle. You'll instead be able to "watch" your thoughts as they arise. You will feel a sensation of opening, as if creating mental space. Indeed, the reason we don't have more peace in our lives is because we crowd it out, externally and internally.

Clearing Your Mind via Observation

Another way to clear your mind is to become aware of your surroundings. Listen to the subtle sounds around you. All silence really is composed of minute amounts of noise. If you are in an office, listen to the ventilation system or the hum of electric lights. It may sound silly, but these can become sacred sounds if you associate them with a calm mind. If you are outside, listen to the sounds of birds and feel the sensation of the breeze on your skin.

Breathe deeply with your eyes open so you can take in your surroundings. Again, don't judge or analyze your surroundings—just notice and accept them. Encouraging yourself to notice details around you is an effective way to quiet your own mind. This is a good practice for a lunch break or a coffee break.

When Your Mind Is Calm

When you find yourself able to calm your mind, you can start consciously observing your thoughts and emotions. If you feel angry or sad about something, think objectively about that emotion and its associated words, images, and feelings. This kind of introspection should be kept free and light. You're *not* psychoanalyzing yourself. You need not form any opinions about the images, opinions, memories, and plans that arise in your mind. Just accept that they're there.

If you find yourself spinning downward in a negative chain of thought, gently bring yourself back to your calm center. If you discover a topic that you really must explore via conscious thought (and these occasions are fewer than you might think), put a bookmark there and return later. Don't waste precious meditation time with outside activity. Right now, your goal is to develop a receptive state of mind in which you attune yourself to your thoughts.

What Are Your Personal Meditation Goals?

People meditate for many reasons: to improve physical or mental health (or both), to develop creativity and intuition, and even to enhance performance on the job or in a sporting event. Knowing why you meditate can help you reach your goals.

Are you a health seeker, a creative thinker, or a performance enhancer? Or are you some combination of these three types? Give yourself the freedom to make an unexpected choice. Perhaps you bought this book to bring more sanity and order into your work life, but now you realize that you're interested in the creative process. Or maybe you came to this book to help address your stress levels, but now realize that you would also like to increase your energy levels. The following chart will help you to clarify your goals. Just look in each column to see which goals most appeal to you. You may wish to highlight or underline the relevant ones, which will give you a personalized meditation blueprint.

Meditation Goals by Type

Health Seeker	Creative Thinker	Performance Enhancer
Lower Blood Pressure	Stop Censoring New Ideas	Improve Memory
Reduce Cholesterol	Work with Greater Flow	Improve Concentration
Reduce Heart Rate	Increase Intuition	Work with Less Distraction
Get Better Sleep	Feel More Connected to Nature and Others	Decrease Self-Criticism
Reduce Anxiety	Sense Divine Guidance or Inspiration	Reduce Workplace Stress
Increase Energy	Visualize Projects	Get Along Better with Others
Improve Immune Response	Release from Past Habits and Memories	Develop Calm Under Stress

Health Seekers

Those who meditate for health benefits are typically easygoing, because they prioritize health over measures of success. They tend to be results oriented (for example, striving for a lower blood pressure reading). Health seekers often already have knowledge of physiology and the body–mind connection, which makes them more receptive to meditation because they understand how it can work.

Yet, they may be so focused on their health goals that they don't realize the potential for self-discovery and spiritual growth. They typically have more difficulty with life organization than performance enhancers, and they may struggle with developing a routine. A big struggle for health seekers is seeing the results of meditation, which accumulate over time and may not be readily apparent in tests immediately.

Creative Thinkers

Creative types take to meditation like fish to water and have no trouble with visualization and other more tangible practices. Meditating in silence can be more difficult for them, and they may have a tendency to dabble too much in multiple styles and routines, which can diminish results. They may also trivialize the everyday benefits of the practice, instead seeking the big, life-altering experiences.

Performance Enhancers

Performance enhancement meditators are the most skeptical of the three types. They often take up the practice reluctantly. Their major challenge is to suspend their disbelief long enough to see some benefits. Once they decide it's important, though, these meditators have little trouble sticking with the practice. The performance enhancer's ability to detect frauds, which are present in the spirituality and natural health fields as they are in all other fields, is a strength and also a weakness. A small dose of skepticism is certainly healthy, but if it goes too far it can shut the door to beneficial practices. While performance enhancers can have trouble dealing with the intangibles of the intuitive mind, they often make up for it with added self-discipline and perseverance.

Knowing Why You Meditate

Knowing why you meditate can keep you focused on the strengths of your particular motivation—yet also make you able to notice your weaknesses and address them. More likely than not, you fall into more than one category, but one will still predominate. All three types of meditators need to persevere, particularly in the beginning, when the practice feels awkward and is not yet incorporated into your daily life. If you can maintain your daily practice for a month or so, chances are, it will stick.

A poker player often has a *tell* that lets other players know when he has a good or bad hand, and the others at the table can use this subtle information against him. Your meditation type is like your tell, the reason you came to meditation in the first place. Your ego will work against you by subtly suggesting that your meditation isn't producing the desired results. That part of yourself that wants to maintain the status quo does not want you to continue to meditate, because that might upset the way things have always been. If you already know that this will happen, you can prepare yourself for it. For example:

- Performance enhancers will hear a voice that says, "You know, you have more productive things that you could be doing . . . ."
- Health seekers will hear a voice that says, "You should probably just exercise and take vitamins . . . ."
- Creative types will hear a voice that says, "This is boring, let's go listen to some music . . . ."

These are just general tendencies, and your particular message will likely be even more specific, tailored to your own life experiences. Your busy mind will come up with a thousand and one reasons not to meditate each and every day. In order to defeat the active, conscious mind, you must be extremely vigilant. You must allow the excuses to arise and dissipate over and over again.

You might also find yourself maintaining the semblance of meditation while at the same time thinking about something else: the committee meeting later in the day, what you're going to make the family for dinner, the evening session in the gym, an unfinished short story or painting. You can maintain two channels in your brain, one that repeats mantras or focuses on a chakra, and another that continues to wander. On one level, this is completely natural and unavoidable. On another level, it means that neither channel is getting your full attention. The challenge is to merge those two streams and go into deep absorption. With time, you will know exactly your own kind of mental wandering, and you will be able to say, "There I go again . . . ." When this happens, take a moment to "watch" whatever thoughts keep intruding (see "Observing Your Thoughts" earlier in this book). Maybe giving them some attention will help you quiet your mind so you can properly meditate.

Where and When to Meditate

Before you begin your meditation practice, consider where and when you will meditate. Look around you for opportunities. For example, a neighborhood park may have a quiet bench for sitting meditation or some secluded paths for walking meditation. Your office building may have a little-used courtyard or conference room ideal for a quick break. That unused study or spare bedroom might become a little oasis, or a porch or veranda might become a hidden refuge from a busy household. Total isolation isn't necessary. Depending on your personality, you may be able to convert even the babble of a crowded train station into the appropriate white noise for meditation.

Now let's examine your daily routine. How can you fit meditation into it? Can you rise thirty minutes earlier in the morning? Fifteen minutes? Ten? Can you claim those first few minutes after arriving at the office, when normally you would browse through e-mails? If you work outside of an office setting, is there a time when you have few customers or clients? Once you start looking for downtimes, you will find them. As you begin to claim them, you will gain more confidence in taking charge of your own time, especially when you see that it enhances your productivity.

Once you have identified places and times for your meditation, you can begin to think about how to use these pockets of tranquility. Following are some common meditation locations and how best to use them.

Meditating at Work

If you have an office with a door that shuts, you have a great scenario for meditating at work. Close the door for a few minutes and don't feel guilty about it. Cut your lunch hour short to make up the time if necessary. If you work in a cubicle, you may not be able to sit on the floor, chant out loud, or light a candle, but you may be able to use headphones to listen to calming music without disturbing your coworkers. If you can't turn off your computer monitor and must sit in front of it, go to an inspiring website (or at least find one that won't be very distracting). If you work on your feet, standing is no particular impediment to the practice of meditation. You will do the exact same exercises while standing, with the added benefit that it will be harder to fall asleep.

If your work environment really is not conducive to meditation at all, you can simply do one-minute to five-minute exercises during the day (maybe during a natural break like a lunch hour) and look for longer periods when you're not at work.

Meditating at Home

Meditating at home often presents just as many challenges as meditating at work. You may feel like you're cheating your family if you take a few minutes to yourself. But practicing meditation will actually make you more attentive to your family, as well as more patient and loving. You will seem more *there* when you meditate regularly, because your mind will not be constantly going off in another direction.

The challenge is finding the right practice at the right time. During a very busy period, you may not be able to do seated meditation. You may only be able to breathe deeply while getting dinner on the table or paying bills at your laptop. Usually, though, you can find a few minutes at some point before bed. This might be after clearing the dinner dishes or putting the kids to bed. You may have to cut back on your television or smartphone time, but odds are you can find some time to work on your meditation.

Gradually, your family will come to understand why you are doing what you are doing, and they, too, will see the benefits as you become calmer and more patient.

Other Places to Meditate

If neither work nor home seems like a suitable location for your meditation practice, think about the other places where you spend time on a daily basis. If you take a train or bus to work, use that time to meditate. If you drive a car to work, practice being mindful while at the wheel: It may save your sanity and even your life!

You could also try meditating while you're running errands. Take one or two minutes to collect yourself in the parking lot before buying groceries. Or duck into a quiet church or library on your way from dropping off the dry cleaning to picking up the dog from the groomer. Use the places that already lie along your route. The loss of time will be more than made up in greater presence of mind.

The Best Time of Day for Meditation

When is a good time for meditation? The diurnal (daily) clock is the one we set our conscious life to, but few are aware of the subtle forces at work each day. At sunrise, your environment is illuminated and natural life awakens. Depending on the time of year and geographic location, the sun may begin to warm the earth, and the temperature arouses certain animal species to either come out into the light or retreat. At noon, the sun is directly overhead, with light and heat at their most intense. Midday is a vital time, and the life force is at its peak. At sunset, the light diminishes as it sinks below the horizon and most active life begins to withdraw. The midnight hour is also a pivotal time of the day, although few are awake to appreciate it.

These four periods are regarded as the "peak points" of the diurnal, or daily, rhythm. The sun is on the east or west horizon, the midheaven (at noon), or the nadir (at midnight). This is how it is viewed both astronomically and in astrology, although each discipline has a different perspective on the meaning. But both agree that these peak points are the vital times of the day and influence human behavior in profound ways.

So when should you meditate? Although the peak points of the day are when you are most ambitious and may want to practice, these times often conflict with other duties. Many people find it most useful to start the day with a morning meditation. By clearing the mind and consciously experiencing stillness, the day does not seem so daunting or ordinary—whichever the case may be. An early evening meditation similarly stills and clears the mind of the day's events.

Whatever time you find best fits your schedule, try to keep it away from mealtimes. If you have not eaten for several hours, a growling stomach may interrupt your meditation session. And if you're meditating right after a meal, the digestive process can similarly be disruptive. Besides, sitting for an extended period right after eating tends to compress the esophagus, bringing on acid reflux or heartburn.

Preparing Your Meditation Space

Think of meditation as the creation of your own oasis, a place where you will refresh yourself. When you first think of an oasis, imagine the dry, lifeless terrain surrounding it. Imagine that terrain to be your current life without meditation. You have journeyed for a long time through this region to reach your oasis, and now you are approaching it. You may be excited to enter this zone, or perhaps you're uncertain. In either case, you've arrived.

Your Meditation Oasis

Select a place where you can begin your meditation practice and continue at your pace, in your own style, without distraction. Ideally this would be a dedicated space that isn't used for anything else, but if that's not possible, you may choose to partition part of a main room with a screen or furniture. If your meditation space will be located outside, make sure you have a comfortable chair, bench, or cushion, and avoid extremes of heat and cold.

Obviously, a place where interference is at a minimum is ideal. You should find a space where the telephone can be turned off and sounds from other rooms can be shut out.

Electronic and electrical equipment can also be a nuisance. At first, the continual hum of a computer fan or the low buzz of a fluorescent light will be distracting when you are starting to focus your attention inward. Make sure you can easily shut down these machines without jeopardizing your safety or comfort.

Removing Distractions

A cluttered space is a distraction. We are often warned against scattering homework or bills on the dining room table or the bed. This is to avoid contaminating the places where we eat and sleep with reminders of stressful or unpleasant tasks. The same goes for your meditation space. Piles of unopened mail and grocery receipts have their own hypnotic power that you may need to escape. An orderly, clean environment encourages the feeling of readiness and ease.

Most of all, your meditation space should not be a place where foot traffic will disrupt your focus. An area where others will be eating, playing video games, or watching television isn't a good choice. Members of your household should not be passing through your space. This will be your sanctuary, so it should offer peace and privacy from the outside world.

Of course, you have to work with the space that you have, and most of us are not lucky enough to have an ideal space in which to meditate. Complete elimination of distraction is neither possible nor desirable, because the annoying elements in our spaces become reminders of why we're meditating in the first place. So strive to have a clean, orderly, inspiring, out-of-the-way place to meditate, but realize that this may never be entirely the case. Even monks and nuns living the cloistered life have physical and mental distractions, which says that these facets of existence can sometimes only be endured or transcended—not eliminated.

Maybe you are fortunate enough to have an exclusive, quiet space that is not frequented by the busy members of your life. Allow as much of the natural environment to prevail. Invite natural light from one or more windows. With so many workers performing their tasks indoors in modern times, the sense of nature's rhythms in the course of both the day and the seasons is seriously diminished. This cuts us off from positive influences and a connection with natural life. Spending time in space with natural light is a good way to counteract these influences and reconnect with the world around you.

Finding the Right Accessories

Your meditation environment should reflect your personal tastes and your goals. You can experiment with this, choosing those elements that suit your personality and home décor. No matter what type of meditation you work with—traditional, secular, or your own eclectic version—you'll need some accessories in the beginning and throughout your meditation practice. Here are some factors to consider:

- **Comfort** is an important concern. You may be spending some time in this space, and you don't want to be discouraged if it feels uncomfortable. You should be able to maintain a comfortable temperature, and keep a warm blanket or throw nearby in case it gets drafty.
- The **wall space** that surrounds you is another consideration. You may want a blank canvas for your initial meditation practice, or you may feel more at ease with the usual décor. Then again, you may want to choose special wall hangings, a set of favorite prints or a calming painting. Many meditators pay great attention to such details in their meditation room, but keep in mind that your approach may change. Because you may be experimenting with different meditation styles in the beginning, an elaborately decorated space may change into a simple one in time.

- **Lighting** is another point to address. Whether you have access to a lot of natural light or depend on artificial sources, make sure it can be adjusted to minimum and maximum levels. Candles are often used for focus in meditation, but they pose safety problems if not used properly. Likewise, incense should be burned in containers that will catch the ashes.

- **Plants and flowers** are other additions to the meditation space that can lend a connection to nature and create a fresh atmosphere. You can even use plants as visual reminders of your meditation practice. Each time you water the plants, you will be reminded that you also need the refreshment of a meditation session. And as the plant grows, so will your proficiency in personal growth and self-awareness.

- **Music** is another consideration. You may want to incorporate background music to get in the mood for meditation, or to balance outside, distracting noises in your house or in the street. You can also find guided meditation and inspirational recordings that are useful as preliminary tools. Look on iTunes for some popular options.

Preparing Your Body for Meditation

Successful meditation does not depend on your ability to contort your body into the traditional "lotus" position of the yogi, sitting cross-legged on the floor. But you do want to be sure your body is in a comfortable and anatomically correct position to ensure a productive meditation.

Your Spine

First and most importantly, your spine should be upright and immobile. This position allows for optimum breathing and less strain on the body overall when you want to maintain one position over an extended period. Besides a practice of proper breathing to aid circulation, the right posture ensures that the entire body can oxygenate and circulate blood without hindrance.

For the spine to be upright, you will be either sitting or standing for meditation practice. For now, we will focus on traditional sitting meditation. Which is best: a comfortable chair or the solid surface of the floor?

Sitting postures require a firm foundation, but at the same time, enough padding should be under you to promote circulation and comfort. Most easy chairs invite slouching and poor posture, but if you have a chair that allows you to sit upright comfortably, feel free to use it. If not, the floor is a good place to begin.

The second consideration is what to do with your limbs. If you are sitting on the floor, should your legs be crossed or folded? Should your feet be tucked under you or at the side? You'll need to do some experimentation here. And, just because someone you know meditates in a perfect cross-legged position doesn't mean you'll be able to do so right away. Keep in mind that circulation is more important than how your position looks. If you plan to sit in a chair, the same guidelines apply. However, your feet must be supported—either by the floor, a footrest, or a cushion.

Try sitting in several different positions. If within five minutes you start to feel numbness in your feet, legs, knees, or bottom, get up and move around for another five minutes. Then try another sitting position. Do this until you find a position that doesn't impose any restrictions or discomfort for at least fifteen minutes at a time.

Your Hands

When you've found your optimum sitting position, what should you do with your hands? You may have seen illustrations of meditating persons with their hands positioned in certain specific poses; these are called *mudras* (Sanskrit for "signs"). They assist in the meditation by focusing the body as well as the mind. But that is a science for later discovery; for now, you want to decide on the most comfortable way to start. If your hands sweat easily, you may want to keep them open, palms up. If they get cold easily, you may want to place them downward, on your lap or knees. Another comfortable position is to place them on your tummy, either folded or with fingers interlaced.

Your Eyes

Your eyes are the third consideration: Will they be open or closed? This is another personal preference, and it depends on the environment you've selected as your meditation space. If the available light helps you become still and relaxed, leave them open. This is the ideal way to begin practicing meditation, so you don't initially confuse the practice with sleeping. Since one of the goals is to raise awareness and harness the mind, using your eyes to notice detail, focus attention, and connect with nature is essential.

If your environment makes it difficult to shut out distractions with your eyes open, close them. When meditating in a group, closing your eyes can help avoid the distraction of others around you.

Basic Meditation Postures

There are three basic postures for meditation: sitting, standing, and prone (lying down). You may find one more comfortable than the others, or you may choose to incorporate some combination of all three into your practice.

Sitting Postures

You have already selected a chair or spot on the floor in the previous section, but how exactly should you sit? For sitting meditation, the lotus posture is viewed as the ideal way to connect the body with the vital energy of earth. Like a lotus, your trunk is akin to the flower's root, grounding itself to the stabilizing force of the land. At the same time, the watery regions of thought and emotion surround you, and the meditation process enables you to float through them unaffected.

Burmese Lotus

The Burmese lotus is so named because it is the sitting tradition of Southeast Asia. The legs are folded, one in front of the other, so that the calves and feet of both legs are resting on the floor. This is a good beginning posture.

Half and Quarter Lotus

For the half lotus, while seated, just one leg (whichever is more comfortable) is folded upward to rest on the opposite inner thigh. The other leg is tucked under the first. This position takes some practice. The quarter lotus is similar to the half lotus, except that instead of resting on the thigh, one leg is resting on the calf of the opposite leg. This posture is easy to negotiate and therefore great for beginners.

Full Lotus

While seated, the legs are folded upward, with the right foot placed on the left hip and the left foot placed on the right hip. The hands rest on the knees.

Standing Meditation

You may find yourself at a time or place where traditional sitting meditation is not possible. If that should be the case, standing meditation is quite effective, although it may not be comfortable for extended periods. As a general rule, any meditation lasting less than fifteen minutes can be done while standing.

Here's how to do it properly: Stand with your spine upright and your shoulders straight. This isn't an extremely rigid military stance, because that would be tiring. Instead, your shoulders should be evenly balanced on both sides. Your chin is tilted slightly upward but not stretched. Stand with your feet about twelve inches apart, in order to balance your weight evenly. Your hands may be placed with palms against your thighs. Or, you may find it more comfortable to hold both hands close to the center of your body, palms inward. Do not cross or fold your arms.

Prone Meditation

Prone meditation is also called lying meditation, and in yoga, *savasana,* or corpse pose. Despite the eerie name, this posture makes it possible to maintain mental and physical stillness while lying down.

Start by choosing a firm surface. If you're on the floor, make sure it is padded enough not to press against portions of the body and cause numbness. If the surface is too comfortable, such as a mattress, it might encourage lethargy and sleep. Try to find a happy medium.

Lie flat on your back, with your spine touching as much of the floor surface as possible. Relax your neck and shoulders, and allow your arms to relax with open palms about six inches away from your body. Look directly up without stretching your neck in any way. If light from a ceiling fixture is too strong, use a floor lamp instead.

Thoughts and Feelings During Meditation

As soon as you establish your time and space and start your first meditation session, thoughts and feelings might begin to rush forward for your attention. Everything you may have put on the back burner in your busy life now comes forward, seeking attention or resolution. This isn't a bad thing—processing your emotions and thoughts is a good byproduct of meditation—but it does take some practice to know how to deal with them in an effective way.

Handling Thoughts

Instead of trying to push thoughts out of the way, you can make a meditation of viewing them in a detached, disengaged manner. You can do this by neutralizing them. Here's how it works: If a distracting thought comes forward, welcome it and ask it to put its case before you. Then listen to what it communicates and return it to the back burner. View it as a disembodied object, like a bubble or cloud. Consider what the thought communicated to you for only a moment, giving it a minimal amount of time, and then allow the next thought to come forward.

For example, let's say you are initiating a new meditation and the thought comes to your mind that you didn't shop for dinner. Ordinarily, you might think of a quick menu, the items you'll need, and, if they're not in the kitchen, when and where you'll buy them. That might lead to remembering that you're almost out of gas, so you'll have to stop before you can get to the grocery store.

Instead, try this. Neutralize the thought by simply acknowledging that you didn't plan dinner yet. Don't assign any blame or judgment. Tell the thought; "I will plan dinner when my meditation is over." Give the thought your attention, assign it a place, and move on.

Processing Emotions

Feelings are a different matter, arising from another realm of your being. Emotions are not amenable to logic, like the thought of planning dinner might be. Feelings may come through the body as sensations, pleasant or unpleasant. They may also appear as attitudes, especially toward yourself. For example, as you begin to sit in meditation, you feel restless, saying to yourself, "Okay, let's get down to business." What does this mean?

Initially, you may feel a wave of impatience, because you procrastinated throughout the day and it's weighing on you. Then you may feel a wave of frustration, reminded that there doesn't seem to be enough time to do everything you want. And finally, a sense of anger may well up, because the interference of others has taken up so much of your time.

Instead, address the impatience with humor. "What's the hurry? I'm here to be free of business." Likewise, meet the frustration with calm, reminding yourself, "The time I give myself will multiply the time I can give to everything else." And always neutralize anger with kindness: "I have been inconvenienced by the interference of others, but now I can make it up to myself." Other feelings may appear when you begin to meditate (for example, hopelessness, discouragement, and other counterproductive feelings). What would you say to a close friend who expressed those feelings to you? You would undoubtedly extend words of hope, encouragement, and motivation. Treat yourself the same way.

Your goal is to balance and settle your emotions—and this is not a quick, easy task. You will need much practice, because you are probably harder on yourself than on anyone else. One attitude to always keep throughout this process is what the Dalai Lama, Tibet's spiritual leader, calls "loving kindness"—tender affection. Practice it on yourself as often as you can.

Delving Deeper Into Thoughts and Feelings

Thoughts and feelings can take turns coming to the forefront in your sessions. If you feel comfortable acknowledging them and returning to your meditation, as explained, you may do so. If you find that particular thoughts and emotions refuse to be put aside, it might be time to spend some time examining them more closely. Asking questions is a beneficial exercise in noticing thoughts and feelings through meditation. This is not a process of analyzing. Rather, it is a way of exercising mindfulness, one of the qualities sought in meditation (you'll learn more about mindfulness in Part III). Throughout the process, you are also bringing forth another innate ability: insight. Together, these dormant tools can provide you with honest, clear answers to all the questions you may have about yourself and your life in general.

When intrusive thoughts or feelings arise, ask yourself the following questions:

- Why do I think/feel this way about that person or situation?
- What causes led to this thought/feeling?

- Why do I still think/feel this way about that person or situation?
- What conditions could make this thought/feeling change?

This is an exercise in "mental housecleaning." And, like regular housecleaning, you can observe yourself doing it. Layers of awareness unfold like the proverbial lotus, and you experience insights along the way.

As you become more adept at acknowledging your thoughts and emotions, an interesting phenomenon begins to happen. The rush of thoughts and feelings subside, and you begin to notice that something else is present—your own awareness, anticipating the next thought or feeling. At that moment, there is a pause in thought and feeling, and it is that pause that you are seeking to cultivate. That is meditation.

Silent Listening As Problem Solving

Once you have established your practice, you can use silent listening as a problem-solving technique. When you have worked your way up to twenty minutes of meditation per session, you can pose a question or problem that you want to solve. To do this, simply ask it: "How can I forgive my spouse for lying to me?" or "How can I resolve the conflict between my new boss and me?" Then set it aside and do your standard twenty-minute practice.

Best Practices

While you can't fail at meditation, you can do certain things to help your practice feel successful and ensure that you stick with it:

- **Try to establish two "anchor" sessions lasting fifteen to twenty minutes, one in the morning hours and one in the evening hours.** This habit makes meditators more likely to stick with the practice. Take shorter meditation breaks during the day.

Optimally, these breaks occur at the same place and time, but this is not strictly necessary.

- **Incorporate deep breathing into your practice—you'll likely see more results than depending on visualization alone.** Deep breathing has physiological effects that complement other forms of meditation. Seeing early results makes it more likely that you will stick with the practice, and because deep breathing exercises are easy to do, they can help you feel more immediately rewarded for your efforts.
- **View your meditation as part of an overall program of well-being.** This means eating a good diet, exercising, and getting regular physical and mental health checkups.
- **Look for like-minded individuals who are also meditating.** Your meditation community could be anything from an online chat room to a temple to a yoga class. These people can help you stay motivated and devoted to meditating.
- **Keep learning and growing in your spiritual life.** You may find it useful to settle on a particular style or school of meditation and receive formal instruction. When you are at the right time in your practice, a teacher will appear who will guide you further down the path. In the meantime, reading books and going to workshops will help keep the practice lively and interesting.

PART II

62 Meditation Exercises

Awakening Meditation

Let your day begin with a few nourishing moments by pausing to meditate. An awakening meditation is an opportunity to ground yourself and create intentions for how you want your day to go, which can positively affect the way things actually go.

Awakening meditations don't have to be complicated or take much time—but do incorporate breathing and stretching if you can. This simple breathing-in-and-out meditation includes positive affirmations to start your day on the right foot.

1. Lie on your back with your arms at your sides in a relaxed manner, or, if you like, place them, palms down, on your stomach so you can feel your breath entering and exiting your body.
2. Begin by stating your intention: "Today is a new day with twenty-four new hours to live; thus I gratefully choose to begin my day with meditation."
3. Then, as you slowly inhale, breathe in this thought: *I vow to start each and every day with an open heart.*
4. Pause briefly, and then, as you slowly exhale, breathe out this thought: *I vow to accept with compassion what comes my way.*
5. Repeat this meditation four or five times.

Throat Chakra Meditation

According to ancient Buddhist beliefs, chakras are wheels of energy that swirl in circles located throughout your body. The seven major chakras proceeding up your spine are: root, sacral, solar plexus, heart, throat, third eye, and crown. Because energy can stagnate in these centers, meditation and yoga often focus on releasing energy or whatever resistance may be clogging your chakras.

The energy located in your throat chakra has to do with personal expression. Taking a moment to open it in the morning will help you express your true feelings, with full power and intention, throughout your day.

1. Sit on the side of your bed, inhale deeply, and as you exhale, stick out your tongue as far as you can and say "Ahhhhhh." Do this forcefully.

2. As you stick your tongue out, notice how the sound emerges. Notice that you can choose to make your words harsh or kind. Sticking out your tongue will relax your throat and stimulate your throat chakra, reminding you to be aware of what you say and how you say it.

3. When your heart and throat chakras are stimulated, you will speak from a place of love and compassion. But not everything in your life will always be sunshine and roses, of course. So take a moment to create an intention for your communication today, such as: *May all of the words I speak today be filled with love, compassion, and truth.*

Ready for Anything Meditation

The first few minutes before *everyone else* gets out of bed can be perfect me-time, when you can declutter your mind with a simple, quick meditation. The idea of this meditation is "nonthinking": emptying all the thoughts that sprang to attention and started marching around your brain the minute you awakened (most of which probably have to do with other people and not yourself). If you take these few minutes to clear your mind, you'll have a much better chance of being able to hear the wisdom of the universe (God, your particular higher power, source of creativity, or divinity). Take at least a few minutes to simply be still and quiet your mind, and the reassurance and energy that you need will come.

1. Choose a place that is clean and uncluttered or, better yet, go to your special meditation space. It's best not to eat anything first, as you want your body to feel comfortable, not busy digesting whatever you've eaten. Plus, meditating first will improve your digestion, and after you have centered yourself, you will be more likely to choose a healthy breakfast.

2. Remove your slippers or socks so your feet can breathe. Those busy feet that take you everywhere have thousands of nerve endings. Those nerve endings stimulate energy and health within your entire body, so give them their due by welcoming them to the meditation and giving them an opportunity to participate.

3. Sit on the floor, drawing in your legs to create a folded, cross-legged posture. If you have trouble crossing your legs in a seated position, slip a folded blanket or pillow under your

hips to help support your back. If this is not comfortable, sit against a wall with your back straight and your legs extended, or sit on a comfortable but sturdy chair.

4. Once you are in this position, slowly straighten your spine, raising the crown of your head toward the ceiling and tucking your chin in slightly.

5. Once your spine is lengthened, relax your shoulders by dropping them down away from your ears and slowly moving your shoulder blades backward, toward each other. Although you want this to be a relaxed posture, it may help to imagine that you are loosely folding your shoulder blades around a grapefruit or a small ball.

6. Close your eyes or just lower your gaze.

7. Relax your hands onto your knees, palms up; or, if you would like, place your hands in your lap, palms up, and then bring your thumb and first finger together to form a *guyan mudra*, a sacred Buddhist symbol in which the thumb represents the soul of the universe and the finger represents your soul. Touching them together represents a union of the two energies, which helps clear your mind, improve alertness, and enhance clarity.

8. Inhale slowly through your nose, and exhale slowly through your mouth. Keep breathing until you achieve a natural rhythm in which the slow intake and slow exhalation are approximately the same length.

9. Spend several minutes doing nothing except focusing on your breath. If thoughts arise, do your best to ignore them, returning your attention to your breath. If it helps, when thoughts arise (and they will), silently acknowledge them but remind your brain that you are choosing to release all thoughts and clear your mind. Soon you'll be able to achieve this without prompts from your mind to your brain.

10. When you feel centered, calm, and grounded in your being, uncross your legs, bring your knees together, slowly roll on your side, wrap your arms around your legs and pull them toward you, giving yourself a hug, and then release and slowly stand. As you move into your day, use your breath as a way to bring your attention back to the feeling you experienced during the meditation, and you should be ready to handle anything life throws your way!

Sippy Straw Exercise

Here's a quickie breathing exercise that will rev up your energy. Many of us are not breathing fully; we have old breath swirling in our lungs. Most of us only use about a quarter of our lung capacity. When you fully exhale, you create space to bring new and fresh breath (*prana*) to the lungs. This full breath will release serotonin and create a feeling of peace.

1. Pretend you are breathing through a straw. Inhale little sips of breath without exhaling. Sip in as much breath as you can. Fill all five lobes of your lungs with breath, until you cannot sip anymore, and then exhale out of your mouth.

2. When you exhale and think you are done exhaling, exhale some more. This is so very energizing that it should not be done in the early evening, as it will keep you awake.

One-Minute Ramp Up Your Energy Meditation

You can still meditate, even if you have just one minute!

1. Stand, with your feet hip-width apart (each foot should be directly under its respective hip), knees slightly bent (also known as *soft knees*, because they're not rigid or snapped to attention as they would be when standing normally). Bring your hands onto your thighs. Inhale, and arch your back, gazing upward, sticking your buttocks out.

2. Then, quickly exhale and round your back, tucking your tailbone and bringing your chin toward your chest. As you move, breathe in and out of your nose forcefully, executing this move quickly. You could do this seven times in just thirty seconds.

3. For the second half of the minute, stand up tall and notice how you feel filled with energy. Breathing in, think: *I have moved my body*. Breathing out, think: *I am energized*. Repeat this several times, and then resume breathing normally.

Fish Pose

Because your mind and your body are interconnected, what you do with your body will make a big difference in your practice of meditation. Yoga makes physical movement a form of meditation. Yoga energizes all of your body's tissues and opens a pathway to vibrant health and spiritual well-being. This is called *fish pose* because it resembles a fish, and because a fish is flexible and strong, capable of moving through water with ease. If you need more flexibility in your life—and who doesn't?—fish pose is a great way to start. Also, if you wake up feeling upset or angry, yoga's fish pose will help you tame your emotions, regain your center, and start your day from a place of love.

1. Lie on your back on a yoga mat or a rug and straighten your legs, flexing your toes upward.
2. Reach your arms down by your sides, and with palms upward, roll from side to side as you take hold of the fleshy part of your upper back legs.
3. Press into your elbows to bend them and use them to lift your chest upward. Let your head drop back (notice that your heart and throat chakras are open in this position). You may want the top of your head to touch the floor lightly. Keep your legs strong and pressing downward.
4. Breathe slowly and deeply through your nose. Visualize your breath going into your heart and your throat and swirling around. Stay in the pose for five breath cycles, or as long as you would like.
5. While in the pose, consciously work on releasing emotions. Let the emotions flood outward. Let this pose be a moving meditation. Breathing in, think: *I am opening my heart.* Breathing out, think: *I am aware of my emotions.*

Forming an Intention

Otherwise known as *creative visualization*, forming an intention for the day (or part of the day) can help guide your mind down the right path.

1. Set a timer for five minutes, do some deep breathing, and allow your mind to reflect on the particular course of action that you would like to achieve. Picture plans falling into place, such as coworkers helping you to achieve your goals, and the complete cooperation of people and circumstances. Put all your mental energy into believing in this ideal vision. Note any resistance or skepticism.

2. When the timer sounds, say a brief prayer for the realization of this vision. When you open your eyes, make a plan on paper for your intention, and stick to the plan as much as possible. You will be surprised by the results.

Mindful Shower Meditation

Whether you shower before breakfast or after, taking a shower provides a few minutes for you to focus on yourself. To take a mindful shower, first clear your mind of any distractions, and then move slowly, enjoying each sensation as it occurs. If it helps, state your intention clearly: "I am shedding all my worries to focus on my body and my senses."

1. Begin by stepping into the shower. How does it feel, going from dry to totally wet? Are the physical sensations pleasant or unpleasant? Stand still for a few minutes, letting the water run over you, quieting all thoughts, experiencing the rejuvenating powers of warm water.

2. Turn your attention to your feelings. How does it feel to have peace and quiet? Breathe in relaxation, and breathe out frustration. Notice as worries dissipate and how it feels when muscle tension subsides. Notice how unadulterated bliss feels in your body.

3. Notice all sensations, such as the fragrance in your soap or shampoo, the grainy texture of your face scrub. Allow the smells and textures to conjure up pleasant memories. Listen to the water as it cascades over your head and hair. What does it sound like? Listen as the drops of water strike the shower curtain or the glass. How does it sound different from when it hits the shower tiles? As steam fills the shower stall, does it make you want to draw swirls on the walls as a small child would? Give it a try!

4. Dismiss all other thoughts. If thoughts about what will happen after your shower or what happened earlier come up, gently brush them aside, and stay focused on sensations

occurring in the shower. Stay fully present, living breath to breath, sensation to sensation.

5. As your shower nears its end, try humming. It not only feels good, but it can sound comforting to you, and to your family if they hear you. Feel the vibrations in your throat as you hum, and attune yourself to this feeling. Often you can recall these sensations later to supersede unkind words you may use throughout the day, particularly if you learn to associate kind words with the feeling of humming. Practice by saying kind words for yourself, such as: "May the words I use to describe myself be loving, kind, and nourishing." Then, state an intention for the day ahead, such as: "May the words I use today, as I talk with my (coworkers, friends, family), be full of love and kindness. May the conversations we share bring us closer together."

6. Toward the end of your shower, take a few really deep breaths, saying "Ahhhhhh" as you exhale.

7. Stay focused on sensations. When you get out of the shower, notice the texture of the towel you use to dry yourself. Notice how it absorbs the water, how clean your dry skin feels against the towel.

8. As you look in the mirror, remember your promise to use kind, loving, and nourishing words when you speak about yourself (and others).

Watching the Breath

All you will do in this meditation is watch your breathing—no more, no less. This breath-watching will, with even a few minutes of practice, calm your nervous system and bring a feeling of peace. With calm breathing, this peace can come very easily and naturally.

Close your eyes. Close your mouth. Take a few minutes to pay attention to your breath:

1. Notice the length of each inhale. If your inhale is only two or three seconds long, you are taking shallow breaths, a surefire sign that you're stressed.
2. Notice the temperature of the breath. Is it cool when you inhale and warm when you exhale?
3. Notice the direction of the breath. When you inhale, can you feel the breath filling your lungs and causing your belly to expand? Can you feel the breath entering your nose and cooling the inside, and then passing downward into your lungs?
4. After bringing all this awareness to your breath as it is, slowly begin to inhale longer and deeper. You want each in-breath to be about five or six seconds long and each out-breath to be an equal length of time.
5. Bring your right hand to your belly. Breathe deeply (five or six seconds), drawing in air until your belly presses into your hand. As you exhale, let your navel sink until it is pressing toward your spine.
6. Continue breathing in and out as you begin to count the breath: 1, 2, 3, 4, 5 for the inhale and 5, 4, 3, 2, 1 for the exhale. If counting seems too boring, say a mantra, such as "May I have peace" as you inhale and "May all have peace" as you exhale.

Three-Part Breath for Good Digestion

This breath will improve digestion, as it is a gentle massage to your abdominal organs. When you inhale deeply, your diaphragm pushes or massages your lower organs, stimulating your digestive tract.

1. Lie down on a yoga mat or a rug. Bring one hand to your abdominal area and one hand to the center of your ribs.
2. This breathing is done with long, slow, deep breaths. Inhale first into your abdomen, and let it expand into your hand. While still inhaling, let your breath expand your rib cage and then expand into your upper chest.
3. Exhale, and let your abdomen soften, your ribs come together, and your upper chest relax. Continue doing this three-part breath for a few minutes.

One-Breath Meditation

Everyday life continually poses challenges to our inner peace. In the midst of a stressful episode, whether at home or at work, we often long for the peaceful moments that a secluded, quiet meditation offers. But the real world doesn't offer such moments when they're most needed; you have to create them. At these times, a conscious pause can refresh your body and mind just as well as an extended meditation session. Just stop and take action—or no action, as the case may be.

1. If you find yourself particularly stressed, feeling that you've come to the end of your rope, stop. Remind yourself that this is an opportune time for momentary meditation, to refresh and relax your mind.

2. Pause all thoughts and remind yourself that your inner peace prevails at this moment. Think of that peace as a place within you. Straighten your spine as you do this, and lift your chin upward. Focus your eyes above your head, at the ceiling or wall.

3. Take a conscious breath, slowly and deliberately. Think of your place of peace opening its door as the air fills your lungs. On exhaling, appreciate the moment for allowing you to pause, and then return to the work at hand.

Breath of Joy

This pose will actually bring a smile to your face!

1. Stand with your feet about one foot apart, with your knees softly bent.

2. Inhale as you raise your arms in front of you to shoulder height . . . inhale some more, opening your arms out to the sides . . . inhale even more, raising your arms overhead . . . and then exhale, saying "HA!" as you swing your arms down toward the ground, bending forward from the hips.

3. Use momentum to swing your arms back up to shoulder height as you bring your body upright, and repeat as many times as you like.

4. Keep going and begin to pick up the speed. Make each "HA!" louder than the previous one. You will find yourself smiling and maybe even laughing!

Eye Cupping

Here's a quick yet surprisingly effective meditation that can be done anywhere when you need to regroup.

1. Cup your hands over your eyes, enough so that you cannot see any light. Close your eyes and feel the darkness for a few slow breaths.

2. While your hands are still cupped over your eyes, open your eyes slowly. This may feel very peaceful. Imagine that you are in the deep shade, in the middle of a forest. Invite peace into your little "cupped" space.

3. When you feel peace entering and feel reassured that you are ready to handle whatever comes, remove your hands.

Mountain Pose

This standing yoga pose is also a good posture for standing meditation.

1. Place your feet together, big toes touching, heels slightly apart. Balance your weight evenly on both feet, with weight distributed across the heels and balls of your feet and your toes.

2. Open your chest by bringing your shoulders down (not up to your ears) and back. Your ribcage will automatically move upward. Move your arms slightly out from your body so that your hands are about six inches away, palms facing forward. Your face should be relaxed, and your head level. Breathe calmly.

Standing Cobra Pose Meditation

Cobra pose is a great energizing pose for the middle of the day. The nature of the movements help release whatever stress or fears have arisen, and restore your energy. And because all you need is a wall, it makes a perfect office break.

1. Stand facing the wall. Place your hands at shoulder height and press them against the wall. Spread your fingers, feeling them press into the wall, and bring your elbows close to your rib cage.

2. Slowly lean forward, until your body is pressed against the wall and your forehead is resting on the wall. (When you press your forehead onto the wall you will be stimulating the third eye, a chakra that is discussed in the next pose.) Take a few breaths with your eyes closed. Inhale and press firmly into your hips. Exhale, lift your heart center as though you want to press it up towards the ceiling, and arch your back, letting your head reach back, opening your throat, and lengthening from your hips all the way up the front of your body. Think about the arch being in the upper back and not the lower back. Keep your neck long and not crunched.

3. Take a few breaths, and then on the exhale, bring your forehead back to the wall. Do this "wall cobra" a few times.

Lying Down Cobra Pose Meditation

This pose is best done when you have some space and some time. It's a good exercise to remind you to breathe deeply into your belly in all meditative situations. Before trying the pose, come up with a mental list of things you can release to make your day run more smoothly. Is there something that you are ready to let go of, maybe a few of the items on your to-do list? Are there a few things you could say no to? Consider these things as you go into cobra pose. As you open into the posture, see yourself rising up to possibilities and to challenges. If cobra pose feels too intense, you may want to try sphinx pose, which is discussed next.

1. Start by lying on your belly on a yoga mat or a rug. Begin with your head turned to one side and your arms relaxed by your sides. Settle your hips by rolling slightly to your right side, rolling your left thigh inward, and then rolling slightly to the left side, rolling your right thigh inward. Pause briefly to rest.

2. As you inhale, allow your breath to go deep into your belly, expanding your belly until it presses into the mat. As you exhale, let your belly pull inward. Exaggerate this breath to create a feeling of your belly doing pushups.

3. Do this pushup breath for a few minutes. When you are ready, bring your forehead to the mat. The area just between your eyebrows and up about an inch is called your *third eye chakra*, which is considered a place of intuition. As your forehead rests, consider whether or not you trust your intuition. How often have you had a feeling about something or someone,

and in retrospect you were correct? Women often have a strong sense of intuition, which can be stimulated by first acknowledging and then focusing, at least briefly, on your third eye during meditations.

4. Next, place your hands, palms down, directly under your shoulders. Your shoulders should be pressing away from your ears and down your back. Pretend you are holding a grapefruit with your shoulder blades, keeping your neck long. With your eyes closed, "look up" to where your third eye is located. This "looking up" will stimulate your sense of intuition, thereby deepening your meditation.

5. Lift up from the crown of your head as you press into your palms and raise your upper body a few inches. See how this feels in your body. If you feel that you can raise yourself higher, keep slowly straightening your arms. If you are strong enough, completely straightening your arms and allowing your bones to support your upper-body weight offers an intense stretch for your back. If it feels too stressful, you can try rolling a blanket and placing it under your pelvis to cushion your pubic and hip bones. If at any time you feel a slight pinch in your lower back, bend your elbows until the pinch goes away. Remember: yoga poses should not hurt.

6. While your shoulders are down, you can try to deepen your meditation. Think of your heart as a flashlight, beaming light on the wall in front of you. Imagine pressing your heart forward (more of an intention than an actual movement) to release love and light into the universe.

7. When you are in the full expression of the cobra pose, breathe in and out of your nose for about five breaths. As you inhale, think: *I am opening.* As you exhale, think: *I am letting go.* If you are gasping for breath, then the stretch has become too intense, and you need to lower your body until your

breath flows more easily and evenly. Holding your breath is another indication that you are too deep into the stretch. As with any yoga posture, if it is more than you can handle you might automatically begin holding your breath. Remember: your breath should be flowing easily and naturally at all times. Don't push it; proceed at your own pace, and the more you practice these stretches, the more limber you will become.

8. After five breaths, lower yourself to the mat, and turn your head to one side to rest. After a moment, you may enjoy releasing any muscle tension in your lower back by slowly "windshield wiping" your feet and legs from side to side. Repeat pose, if desired.

Sphinx Pose Meditation

This is very similar to cobra pose and has many of the same benefits as cobra—but it is much gentler.

1. Lie on your belly on a yoga mat or rug. Come up on your elbows, palms down, with your fingers pressing down and pointing straight ahead. Your legs are straight behind you, and your thighs are rolled in; the fronts of your thighs are moving toward each other and the backs of your thighs are moving away from each other.

2. Relax your buttocks and legs to open up your lower back. Feel your pelvis drop into the mat or rug.

3. Close your eyes and take a few slow breaths. When you are done, bring your elbows down and to the sides and rest your head to one side. Stay resting for a few more breaths.

Walking Meditation

Walking meditations are nothing if not blissful, particularly if you live in a beautiful area or have access to rivers or ponds or woods. They present the perfect occasion to be alone in your thoughts. Walking meditations can help you release the nagging stream of thoughts clattering and clanging around in your mind, by surrendering to the simplicity and beauty around you—such as noticing the tiniest, loveliest, most serene details of a natural stream. Still, the best part of a walking meditation is that you can do it almost anywhere—simply strolling around the block will do.

1. Before you begin a walking meditation, pretend that you have never walked before. It helps to practice in your home with bare feet before trying this one outdoors. Create a clear path, maybe a hallway, or any place in your home where you can walk back and forth. Begin by focusing on your posture, straightening your spine from your tailbone to the crown of your head, standing squarely over your feet and hips. Feel your feet on the floor. Pretend that your feet have never touched or felt the floor, like you're on another planet and have no idea how this "new ground" will feel. Feel every inch of your feet touching the floor . . . each of your toes, the bottoms of your feet, and your heels. Feel the texture and the coolness of the tile or wood, or the cushioning of the rug. Be curious about how everything feels under your feet. Lengthen your body up through your spine to the crown of your head. Bring your shoulders down and back to open your heart center. Make sure your chin is slightly tucked.

Take small steps, and step lightly and slowly. Smile while you are walking. Realize how different it is to walk without having a place to go and how refreshing it feels to be focused solely on walking, surrendering all thought about anything other than walking. Now you are ready.

2. Pick a place that you would like to walk—by a stream, on a path in the woods, by a fence. You can even have a walking meditation on a busy city street, but it will be more difficult and require more concentration. Keep in mind that you have no destination, just walking . . . that's it. Let go of any worries or concerns as you walk. Keep a smile on your face. Slow your walk to a stroll. This is not "power walking." Let go of any agenda about walking, and focus on noticing the beauty of your surroundings. See things as if for the first time, as if you have been blind all of your life and now you can see. Notice all of the beauty that you see, from clouds in the sky to veins in a leaf, and really look at everything, surrendering all judgment. Let go of having to arrive anywhere and simply focus on enjoying the process of walking, surrounded by light and air and beauty.

3. Remember that this is a meditation, which means you want to keep returning your focus to your posture and your breath. As with any meditation, your breath should be slow, rhythmical, and drawn deeply into your belly before being fully expelled. Maybe inhale for two steps and exhale for two steps. Focus on the rhythm until it feels natural, and then bring your focus back to the beauty and the simple process of walking, affirming that you are walking all of your cares and worries away.

4. Walk as long as time permits, and end your walk by pausing to take a few cleansing breaths. If you like, you can bring your hands into prayer position and pause to express your

gratitude for the beauty of your surroundings. Notice how peaceful and quiet your mind has become, and remember this feeling so you can tap back into it when things begin to pick up speed. Notice what thoughts are first to appear. The more you learn to quiet your mind and let go of any thinking, the more surprised you'll be when insights start popping up toward the end of your walk.

Rebalancing Meditation

Tree pose is perfect physically and psychologically for dealing with re-entry stresses—such as going back to work on a Monday or readjusting to life after a vacation. It helps develop balance, steadiness, and poise.

1. Stand with your feet hip-width apart. Feel the four corners of each foot pressing evenly into the floor or ground. (This is a great meditation to do outside with bare feet, weather permitting.) Lengthen your spine, and lift the crown of your head toward the ceiling (or the sky, if practicing outside). Feel all of the muscles wrapping around your legs. In other words, gently engage your leg muscles, especially lifting the quad muscles; lift your pelvic floor by pulling up the muscles as though you were trying not to pee, and engage your abdomen by pulling the stomach muscles inward.

2. Bring the sole of your right foot to the inner thigh of your supporting leg (your left leg), and open your knee out to the side. (Feel free to touch a chair or wall to help with balance.) Bring your hands together in a prayer position. Look at something that is not moving to help with balance, and focus on your breath until you feel steady. When you feel steady, bring your hands up as though you were extending your branches. While in tree pose, think about what tree you resonate with today. Are you a willow tree, swaying back and forth, or are you an oak tree, standing firm and strong? How about a cherry or apple tree?

3. If you are not able to balance today, use this as an opportunity to reflect on what may be out of balance in your life. As you do balancing postures, you may notice that some days you can balance for quite a while and other days not so much. Being mindful is noticing (without judgment) the differences from day to day.

Cleanse Your Energy

If you've been around people whose negative energy has rubbed off on you, take an energy-cleansing "shower"!

1. Stand and imagine you have removed your clothing. Inhale and reach your arms up.
2. Exhale and lower your arms to your sides, imagining a shower of sparkling gold light trickling over your body.
3. Repeat the motion several times, allowing this gold light to cascade over your body and clean all of the negative energy you may be feeling or may have picked up during the day. Visualize the negative energy flowing away from you and being absorbed by the earth.

Clearing Obstacles

When your plans aren't coming together, when you're feeling frustrated and ineffective, it's best to take a short break instead of plowing ahead. This is especially powerful for work settings.

1. Sit up straight in your chair, breathe deeply for three cycles, and picture a particular problem clearly in your mind's eye. If the problem has a lot of emotion attached to it, breathe into the raw emotions in order to soothe and clear them.

2. Take a look at the problem and picture it being solved: a friend coming to offer advice, a coworker taking up the slack, last-minute inspiration occurring, a client satisfied with your work. See the work finished in the best possible way, and take some time to enjoy this feeling.

3. Continue breathing deeply, and return to work in a calmer and more confident state of mind.

Dismissing Thoughts

Sometimes you find yourself inundated by negative thoughts. When that happens, try this calming meditation. It allows you to acknowledge your thoughts and then dismiss them, freeing up space for positive thoughts to enter your mind.

1. Sit in your meditation space, either in a straight-backed chair or cross-legged on the floor. Close your eyes and begin breathing deeply: eight counts in, hold four counts, eight counts out, hold four counts. Keep counting your breaths for four to six cycles. When you can maintain the same rhythm, let go of the counting.
2. Watch your thoughts. As they arise, dismiss them, silently saying, "Not this" or "Not that." Keep your negation simple without attaching any emotion or aggression to it. At the same time, keep your attitude expectant, as though you were waiting for something better than the thoughts your mind normally presents to you.
3. Continue dismissing your thoughts, one by one, for the rest of the session. Don't worry if you have trouble doing this; just keep trying. When you open your eyes, note any shifts in your perceptions.

Hidden Community

If you usually practice meditation alone, take a few moments to remind yourself that there are thousands of other people around the world learning meditation, too. Embracing this community will allow you to share your positive energy and will keep you motivated.

1. Practice deep breathing for five minutes, on the pattern of inhaling for twelve counts, holding for six, exhaling for twelve, and holding for six. During this time, picture your inner self opening to the cosmos: expectant, loving, and serene.

2. During the second five minutes of this meditation, think of the others around the world struggling to establish themselves in the practice of meditation just as you are. Perhaps even take one minute to think of those who are reading this book, doing these exercises, just like you. Send these fellow travelers the same positive energy that you have experienced in your meditation. Wish them success in all of their material and spiritual endeavors. Picture their physical bodies healed of any health conditions, and wish them vibrant health and longevity. See their questions answered, their problems solved. Know that others are wishing the same for you, and feel this hidden support for all that you do.

3. When the time has expired, consider reaching out to others on the path of meditation through a web posting, e-mail, or phone call.

Child's Pose

In yoga, child's pose serves as a resting place between other more challenging poses, but it also makes a comfortable position for meditation.

1. Come to your hands and knees. Inhale deeply, and when you exhale, lower your hips down to rest on your heels and flatten the tops of your feet on the floor. You can stretch your arms out above your head so that your palms rest on the floor, or you can stretch your arms straight down by your sides, palms up. Either way, close your eyes and keep your forehead gently resting on the floor.
2. Use this time to rest, recharge, and focus on your breath. When you are finished, come out of the pose slowly, coming back to hands and knees for a moment before rising.

In-Out Meditation

This meditation is simple and traditional. When you have a particularly busy day ahead, this very easy practice can clear your mind without requiring much mental exertion. Learning to quiet your mind and focus on your breath is key to mindfulness, and you may enjoy this place of "non thinking" so much that you will want to remain in this meditation for longer periods of time.

1. Sit in a comfortable posture on your floor, rug, or yoga mat.
2. Lift your hips a tiny bit so that your knees are in alignment with your hips. If necessary, place a small pillow or a rolled towel under your hips.
3. Lengthen your spine and bring your chin toward your chest so that the crown of your head is reaching upward.
4. As you slowly breathe in, say, "In."
5. As you slowly breathe out, say, "Out."
6. If your mind wanders, gently but firmly bring it back to focusing solely on the In-Out breath. Replace your thoughts with your breath. Stay for five minutes to start, and work your way up to ten minutes.

Object Meditation

If you've spent a lot of time lately helping others, this meditation can help bring your focus back to you. Find an object that is beautiful or interesting to you. It can be a shell, stone, a religious icon, a piece of jewelry—anything that is meaningful to you.

1. Place the object in front of you, positioned so that you can sit and gaze forward at it.
2. Keep your eyes focused on the object without looking away.
3. Begin to breathe deeply, transitioning into long, slow breaths that you draw deeply into your belly, slowly and fully.
4. Keep your every thought on the physical aspects of the object—the texture, size, color . . . . All awareness rests on the physical aspects of the object. When your mind wanders, notice what it wanders to, and then bring it back to the object.
5. Once you feel calm and focused, close your eyes and try to "see" the object in your mind's eye. If you lose your concentration, open your eyes, study the object, and then try again.

Stay with this meditation for five minutes, or as long as you'd like.

Going with Gravity

Being pulled in a dozen different directions by people, work, and responsibilities can take a toll on you, physically and mentally. This meditation reminds you to reconnect with the natural forces that are in play around you, all the time.

1. Find a place where you can lie flat on the floor without being disturbed. Turn off the light (if you can). If you feel any discomfort, place a cushion beneath the small of your back, behind your knees, or under your neck.

2. Set a timer for five minutes. Practice deep, slow breathing. Become conscious of gravity pulling your body into the floor. Imagine gravity pulling any tension out of your body and pulling away disturbing thoughts as well. Become one with the floor beneath you, and imagine yourself to be an inanimate part of the floor. Pretend that you have forgotten how to speak, either to yourself or out loud.

3. Allow yourself to rest in a state as close to mindlessness as you can achieve. When the timer sounds, try to take some of this interior silence with you.

Metta (Loving Kindness) Meditation

Metta meditation is a way to bring about intimacy first with yourself and then with others. The Buddha was precise about the myriad benefits of this meditation and proclaimed that:

- You will sleep easily.
- You will wake easily.
- You will have pleasant dreams.
- People will love you.
- Devas (celestial beings) and animals will love you.
- Devas will protect you.
- Poisons, weapons, and fire (external dangers) will not harm you.
- Your face will be radiant.
- Your mind will be serene.
- You will die unconfused.
- You will be reborn in happy realms.

Sounds worth trying, right?!

1. To begin, come to a quiet place, and breathe slowly, until you begin to feel calm.
2. State this wish for yourself: "May I be happy and free from suffering." As you say these words to yourself, acknowledge all of your goodness.
3. Think of someone you have strong respect and gratitude for, and visualize him or her as you state this wish: "May Jonathan be happy and free from suffering." Next, think of a close friend and say: "May Paula be happy and free from suffering." Think of a neutral person, someone you do not know very

well, such as the barista at your local coffee shop or the UPS delivery person, and state: "May my UPS delivery person be happy and free from suffering." Think of a difficult person, someone whom you do not like, and state: "May Harold be happy and free from suffering." This can be challenging. Maybe bring that person to mind and linger for a while, thinking about others whom you also do not like. Do not force or even try to manufacture disingenuous feelings of any kind, such as affection for someone whom you do not like. Just say the words as though the words were delicate glass sculptures, and in doing so, you may feel more loving toward that person and toward *all beings*.

4. End the Metta meditation by thinking of *all beings*, and state: "May all beings be happy and free from suffering."

Warrior Pose

A true warrior has strength and wisdom and a strong heart. A warrior celebrates another's victory with generosity. It's not about who wins; it's about being strong enough to compete with honor and both win and lose gracefully. It's about honoring your opponents and yourself—win, lose, or draw.

1. Start with your feet hip-width apart.
2. Inhale and place your hands on your hips.
3. Exhale, step your left foot back, bend your right knee, and allow your body to sink down through your sitting bones. Press back through the heel of your left foot.
4. Inhale and raise your arms upward, bringing them perpendicular to the floor and parallel to one another. Reach your arms as high as you can to stretch your ribcage. While continuing to breathe, hold this pose for 30–60 seconds.
5. To release, lean forward and bring your left foot up to meet the right. Bring your hands back to your hips.
6. Take a few breaths, and then do the other side.

Corpse Pose (Savasana)

Taking a restorative midday "nap" can help you reduce stress and stay healthy and available for your family. The purpose is not to really sleep, but to rest your body and mind. A savasana nap has the added benefit of reminding you to be mindful as you relax and refresh yourself. Savasana typically is practiced at the end of a yoga session as a way to rest the muscles (and the mind!) while allowing the poses just completed to work their magic, but it's also a great way to quiet your mind and body and practice a refreshing silent meditation.

1. Corpse pose, or savasana, is done while lying flat on your back on a yoga mat or a rug. Many find it more comfortable to place a bolster, rolled towel, or pillow under their knees. A folded hand towel or a scented eye pillow placed over your closed eyes will help you relax further. Some people like to play soothing instrumental music while taking a savasana rest.

2. To begin, bring your arms straight down by your sides. If you are cold, bring your arms close to your body, and if you are warm, move your hands about several inches or more away from your sides. If you wish, using a light blanket can feel comforting. Remember, the intention is not to fall asleep but to remain alert in your mind and very still in your body, which is surprisingly relaxing, particularly if you maintain the pose for a good ten minutes or slightly longer.

3. When you feel rested (or when your music or timer cues you that the time is over), roll to your side, come up slowly, pause to take a few deep, cleansing breaths, and then open your eyes.

If you *do* want to take an actual nap after spending some time in corpse pose, here's what to do:

1. Notice how your heart and breath slow down. Notice the noises outside of your home—maybe the wind or rain, maybe cars or trucks driving by, a neighbor's dog, or children playing in the distance. Just notice and breathe, listening to the sounds of life.

2. Now bring your awareness inside the house, and notice all the interior sounds, such as the humming of a heater, air conditioner, or maybe a fan. Listen to all of these sounds while breathing slowly and rhythmically.

3. Bring your awareness to the sounds of your own breath, how it sounds smooth and relaxed. Bring your awareness even deeper. Can you hear vibrations? Can you hear humming? Stay with this humming, and let it soothe you into rest.

4. When you are ready to end your nap, give yourself a few minutes. Deepen your breath, become aware of your surroundings, and begin to wiggle your fingers and toes. Turn your wrists and ankles in circles. Turn your head gently side to side, slowly waking up your body. After a few breaths, reach your arms overhead, inhale deeply, and say "Ahhhhh" as you exhale. Roll both of your legs to the side and slowly push up to a sitting position. When you are ready, begin the next part of your day refreshed.

Fold Over Pose

In our culture, we tend to hold a lot of tension in our hips (and shoulders), creating tightness in our lower backs. When you open your hips in this posture, it will also open your lower back and release that tension. If you don't mind looking a little silly, this is a posture you can practice on a bench while watching your child's soccer practice.

1. While seated in a chair or on a bench, cross your right ankle over your left knee. Feel both of your hip bones pressing down evenly on the seat. Inhale, filling up your lungs. As you exhale, fold forward until you feel your right hip and buttocks release and open up. Place your arms on the inside of the calf of your right leg, folding one palm over the other. Let your back relax into the fold. You want to be at an edge, meaning that you want to feel this strongly but not painfully. The point just before pain begins is a good, strong edge.

2. Once you feel your edge, commit to staying still for at least three minutes and as many as seven. During this long hold, try to relax all of your muscles and let the tug be deep inside your joints. Breathe evenly. If you are holding your breath or gasping, you are too deep into the stretch and need to back off. If possible, let your eyes close and become aware of all of your physical, emotional, and mental sensations. Do not judge what may come up for you. Just notice with curiosity, and let the sensation go.

3. After a few minutes, switch sides.

Twisting Pose

This spinal twist loosens your midsection and neck. Remember to keep your breathing slow and steady.

1. Sit up tall on a chair or bench. Sitting at the edge will help lengthen your spine. Bring your chin slightly toward your chest to lengthen the back of your neck.
2. Inhale deeply, and then exhale saying "Haaaa," letting your breath fall away. Repeat a few times.
3. Begin to breathe in and out of your nose, slowly and deeply.
4. Inhale. Then, as you exhale, bring your left hand over to your right knee, draping it around your knee, if comfortably possible.
5. Turn your head to gaze over your right shoulder.
6. Bring your right hand behind you, and press down on the seat for leverage to help you to keep your spine erect.
7. Stay for a few minutes, and then switch sides.

Straight-Leg Forward Bend

This meditation will help you release worry. Some days, you may find that even this meditation doesn't work—your worries just won't go away. That's okay, too. Simply *accept* the worries as they are. With practice, it will become easier to let the leaf float downstream.

1. Sit up straight on the edge of a chair or bench.
2. Inhale through your nose, and exhale saying "Haaaa."
3. Breathe deeply through your nose, or through your mouth if that's not comfortable.
4. Straighten your legs in front of you, and flex your feet by pressing your toes toward your forehead; feel your hamstrings stretch.
5. Lean forward without bending your knees. Come to your edge, that point just before pain begins, and stay for a few minutes.
6. Try closing your eyes. Notice any physical, emotional, or mental experiences you may be having, such as experiencing a tight hamstring, or feeling overwhelmed, or worrying about something happening in your workplace. Each time a thought or emotion surfaces, try to replace it with a breath. Or, you can envision a stream and picture each thought or sensation or emotion as a leaf floating by. For example, you may be in your posture and realize that you are planning dinner in your head. Look at this thought, and let it float by. You might begin reliving an argument you had with a family member. Notice this, thinking, *Oh, rather than obsessing over this fight, I'm going to let it float down the river.* This leaf floating of sensations and thoughts becomes a mindfulness meditation (see Part III). Some people also picture troubling thoughts or emotions as butterflies that flit easily into the atmosphere.

Backbend

Here's another meditation that will help you release tension in your back. It can be especially useful midway through a long day at the office.

1. Sit at the edge of a chair or bench.
2. Inhale through your nose, and exhale saying "Haaaa." Repeat a few times.
3. Inhale and reach your arms forward, clasping your hands and interlacing your fingers.
4. With your fingers interlaced, turn your palms away from you.
5. Round your spine and bring your chin to your chest.
6. Exhale and reach upward, keeping your fingers interlaced. Look up (but do not crunch the back of your neck).
7. Arch your back. Think of your heart center reaching forward and lifting upward. In other words, you are arching more in the upper back than anywhere else.
8. Reach as far as you can, and stay for a couple of minutes.
9. Come forward again, rounding your spine.
10. Do this a few times. Always come slowly out of any back bend, and round your spine to release any tension.

Stirring the Pot Meditation

This meditation allows you to think about the past in a healthy way. With practice, you'll become more adept at letting old memories go and creating new visions for your future.

1. Sit on the floor or a yoga mat. If it would feel more comfortable, place a folded blanket or small pillow under your hips. Cross your legs, and bring your hands down onto your knees. Pretend you are sitting on a big clock.

2. Lean over toward your right knee, and circle your upper body over toward your left knee. Continue circling around until you make a big circle going in a counterclockwise direction.

3. Inhale as you round forward, gently sticking out your chin.

4. Then, exhale as you round back, bringing your chin toward your chest.

5. As you are "stirring the pot," think back in your past. You are going counterclockwise! Think about something that hasn't worked out for you. Can you let this memory go?

6. Keep going around for a few minutes. What else comes up for you in your past?

7. Now reverse directions, and this time close your eyes and look up toward your third-eye point (the place between and above your eyebrows). Think about what you would like to see in your future.

8. As you continue rotating in a clockwise direction, pretend you have a great big canvas and you are going to create a work of art. This work of art will embody what your heart's desire is. Take as long as you want in creating this imaginary

canvas. You can use imaginary paint, pen, photos, or anything that your creative imagination comes up with.

9. After you are finished creating a vision of your heart's desire, stop and "study" it with your eyes closed. What do you see? What is your third eye "telling" you?

10. When you feel ready, slowly open your eyes, retaining a clear memory of what your heart most wants to have happen.

Pelvic Tilt

Your midsection can get very cramped if you sit for long periods of time during the day. Try this pose to realign your body at your lunch break.

1. Stand with your feet slightly more than hip-width apart, keeping your knees slightly bent. Inhale and bring your hands to your knees.
2. Exhale as you round your spine, bringing your chin to your chest. Tilt the bottom of your pelvis forward. Inhale as you reverse this position. Arch your back, look up, and stick your chest out.
3. Continue tilting and arching for about three minutes.

The Cave of the Heart

As you go along in your busy day, it can seem impossible to find a quiet moment *anywhere*. If you're feeling that way, try this meditation. It reminds you that you carry a shrine within you wherever you go: in the cave of your heart.

1. Sit up straight, either cross-legged on the floor or in a chair with your feet on the floor. Begin by breathing deeply, concentrating your awareness between the eyes. When you have entered fully into a rhythm of deep breathing, observe your internal space, the darkness before your eyes. You may see subtle lights, like electric sparks floating around. You may see mental formations, such as words and images, or you may see the outlines of your body or the room in which you are sitting.

2. Gradually move your center of awareness downward along your spinal column, until it rests in the center of your chest. This may be a little difficult, because many people think of the head as the seat of consciousness. With a bit of effort, you should be able to remain in the chest region. Now begin to see this space. You may sense darkness, or you may visualize your heart and lungs expanding and contracting.

3. Now allow this area to fill with a white light tinged with violet. Picture this light as a countervailing force against the words and images in your head, just as the sun breaks through rain clouds after a storm. Make this inner vision stronger, until the light is extremely powerful.

4. After the visualization is established, stop trying to consciously produce it. Go back to simply observing. Realize that light and darkness are not opposites but part and parcel of the same reality.

Sacred Wounds

This meditation helps to release past hurts that may prevent you from expressing your full potential. You may have some traumatic experiences that have always lingered in the shadows because you were not capable of releasing them. These old wounds may make you overly cautious in some areas, or prevent you from developing emotional connections with others. As you go through this exercise, be gentle with yourself. Don't try to force yourself to let go of something before you are ready. Let your heart progress as it will. Deep breathing and visualization work will help. As you realize your own boundless power, the hurts of the past will seem less and less consequential. You may never forget what has happened to you in the past (and you probably shouldn't), but those past events will cease to have a strong hold on you.

1. Bring awareness to your heart center through deep breathing and close observation. Feel your heart beating in your head, the rush of blood through your arteries and veins. See how the heart nourishes and enlivens your whole body. See it not only as an organ, but as the essence of yourself, spreading beneficent energy to your whole self: body, mind, and spirit.

2. Now go into a diligent listening mode. Ask your heart to reveal its wounds to you, the ways it has been hurt in the past that prevent your growth from going forward. Don't force the issue. If nothing comes to you, do not try to make the experience happen. You can always try again later.

3. Some scene from your past may appear in your mind's eye: a coworker who criticized you, a former lover who left

you, a public embarrassment of some kind. Be prepared for something unexpected that you buried deep inside. Simply notice this wound from the past and acknowledge it. That may be as far as the exercise goes for now.

4. If you feel ready (and only if you feel ready), speak into that wound. Say to your past hurt, "I am ready to let you go. I forgive those who were responsible, I forgive myself, and I am ready to turn this wound into a source of strength." Picture the same radiant energy that pulses through your body washing over your wounded heart.

5. When you are finished with the exercise, your heart will still bear its wounds, but the scars will be healed to a greater degree than they were before. Particularly deep wounds may require multiple sessions.

Honor Your Inner Child, Meditation #1

Here's the first of two opportunities to visit your inner child. After you have reconnected with your inner child, you can move on to honoring the person you have become. For this meditation, find a quiet place to sit, and close your eyes.

1. Breathe slowly until you begin to feel calm. (Never worry if you are not able to get to a calm place. That will come with time and practice.)

2. Think back to when you were a child. Try to remember a time when you were not feeling acknowledged or loved. See if you can remember the circumstances and what led to those feelings. Try to see yourself as a child in the memory. Embody the memory by remembering little details, like what you were wearing, what time of year it was, or who else was present.

3. During this process, keep your breath long and even, returning focus to your breath as needed. If the memory is really difficult or painful, you can choose not to go there and try another memory instead.

4. With your eyes remaining closed, "look" into the eyes of the child (that was you) and visualize wrapping your arms around her and talking softly with her. If she is crying, let her continue to cry while you hold her. If you begin to cry, let the tears flow.

5. When you both feel more composed, gently ask your inner child to tell you why she feels left out or unloved. Listen intently, allowing her feelings to wash over you.

6. When the story feels complete, tell her you are sorry that she felt this way in the past. Reassure her that you love her and want to make her happy.

7. Say farewell to her, and after a moment of resting in silence, go back to focusing on your breath. Inhale memory . . . exhale acceptance and love.

8. Continue breathing until you feel re-energized.

Honor Your Inner Child, Meditation #2

Another meditation that can help you honor your inner child involves happy memories!

1. Breathe slowly in and out until you feel calm.
2. Think back to when you were a child, to a time when you were feeling good about yourself, and happy.
3. Remember any details, like what you were wearing and who was with you. Why were you feeling so proud or joyful?
4. See yourself as that happy child, and move closer so you can be with her and share the happy moment.
5. Notice how it feels to re-experience childlike joy. Can you bring that feeling into your life right now?
6. Stay with this experience, breathing slowly in and out, until you feel very happy and ready to come out and play!

Listen to Your Intuition Meditation

When you are able to keep your thoughts in stillness for a few minutes, you will be able to tap into your intuition.

1. Sit cross-legged on a folded blanket.
2. Make sure that your spine is lengthened.
3. As discussed in Part I, before you begin your meditation practice, it is nice to set an intention. (An intention can be thought of as a prayer.) For example, your intention might be to have peace in your heart and peace with all the relationships in your family.
4. After you formulate your intention, close your eyes, and relax your jaw by parting your teeth. Only your lips will be touching.
5. Bring your hands, palms facing upward, onto your knees. (This hand gesture expresses the intention of receiving wisdom from the universe—or from God, if you prefer.)
6. Anchor your breath to a phrase, such as something from your intention.
7. Inhale. Think, for example, *May I have peace within my heart.*
8. Exhale. Think, for example, *May I have peace with all the relationships in my family.*
9. As you breathe, keep repeating your intentions.
10. Try this for as long as twenty minutes if you are able. Set a timer so you won't be distracted with watching a clock.
11. After the timer goes off, sit in stillness, recognizing that an intention is powerful and that you can have faith and trust in the process. Notice how calm you feel, and savor this moment.

Releasing Shoulder Tension Meditation

Tension can build in your shoulders, just as it can in your back. If you're feeling weighed down—literally, after a big grocery store trip, or metaphorically—try this tension-releasing meditation.

1. Bring yourself to a comfortable seated posture on the floor with a folded blanket or towel to sit on.
2. Inhale for a count of five, and exhale for a count of seven. Your breath is creating space. You are not able to bring new things into your life until you let some things go.
3. Stay with this breathing until you are feeling calm (or at least calmer than before).
4. Have the intention of letting some things go.
5. With your eyes closed, notice how you are feeling in your physical body. Notice if you feel tension in your shoulders. Do you hold the weight of the world on your shoulders?
6. With your eyes closed, think about who or what is on your shoulders, causing you to feel weighted down. You may have your entire family lined up on your shoulders. Picture all of them lined up. What else or who else is there? Friends, aging parents, work responsibilities? Take time to really notice all of the people and "stuff" you are carrying.
7. Inhale into your belly.
8. Exhale slowly; as you lean to your right, reach your right arm straight out and tilt over until your fingertips touch the floor.
9. Watch as everything and everyone slides off your shoulders, joyfully "listening" as they scream "Wheeeee" while soaring

down the slide that is your arm. Let them slide off, trusting that they will be fine, that they don't need to rest on your shoulders.

10. Inhale into your belly.

11. Exhale slowly, and repeat the same motion with your left arm, letting everything and everyone on that side slide off. You may have to shake your arm, as some people will (consciously or unconsciously) hold on really tight, even if everyone (especially you) knows it's good to let them go.

12. You have created space with your exhale being longer than your inhale. You have also let quite a few things go. You can now fill up with calm, peace, joy, or whatever it is that you need.

13. When you fully exhale, you have given all that you can. There is nothing more than to have faith in your next inhale.

Gas-Relieving Pose

This posture will stimulate your abdominal organs and digestive tract. If you do this every day, it can help restore and maintain digestive health. This posture also gently stretches your lower back and keeps your vertebrae aligned.

1. Lie on your back on a rug or yoga mat. Press your heels down, lengthening as you flex your feet, creating a nice stretch for your back and hamstrings. Inhale, bringing your breath down into your belly. As you exhale, bring your right knee up toward your chest.

2. Wrap your fingers around the front of your knee. Continue breathing deeply. As you inhale, release your knee slightly, and as you exhale, draw your knee firmly toward your chest, keeping your extended left foot flexed (toes pulled toward your forehead). Repeat a few times with your breath. This movement will massage the ascending colon. (Always start with the right knee, as this is the direction of movement in the colon.)

3. Reverse sides. Bring your left knee up toward your chest, and wrap your fingers around the knee. Breathe deeply. As you inhale, slightly release the hold on your left knee, and as you exhale, draw the knee firmly toward your chest. This will stimulate the descending colon. Keep your extended right foot flexed. This is very effective and should be done for several minutes.

4. When you are done with both sides, bring both your knees up toward your chest and wrap your arms around your knees. Give yourself a big hug, and gently roll from side to side.

Giving Thanks Meditation

The more you practice being grateful, the easier it will come to you. Done often, it can become an extremely rewarding habit. Before you start this meditation, light a candle, recognizing that you can *choose* to focus upon and experience thankful energy flowing throughout your body, appreciation for your place in the universe, and a joyful feeling for your current life situations.

1. Sit quietly, and breathe in and out slowly, until you quiet your mind and feel relaxed.
2. Visualize, in as much detail as you are able, people whom you are grateful to have in your life. Begin with those you love, and then extend your gratitude to anyone who has crossed your path in life and positively impacted you.
3. Visualize things that you are grateful to have in your life: your senses, blue sky, cool breezes, red wine, lobster, family, laughter, starry nights, full moons, vivid colors, music, washing machines, vacuum cleaners, fireplaces, or whatever comes to mind.
4. Visualize qualities you have that you are grateful are part of your total being: persistence, dedication, cheerfulness, intelligence, and so on. Bring your hands to a prayerful pose against your heart, and offer thanks for your many blessings.

Teatime Meditation

In the midafternoon, take a moment to indulge in a refreshing cup of tea—and do a mindfulness meditation while you're at it.

1. Teatime meditation is about using all of your senses. Use your favorite teacup or even use your good china for teatime. Why not? Pampering yourself adds to the relaxation and refreshment you derive from a mindful meditation.

2. Pour the water into a teapot or directly into your cup. Let it sit for a few minutes. Lean over and smell the scent of the tea. Look at the color of the tea. Is it gold? Think about the color of gold. What does this bring up? Stay with positive thoughts: flecks of gold in your child's eyes, the gold of a sunset or a summer flower, a gold wedding ring, or anything that comes up.

3. Deeply inhale the scent of the tea and bring the cup up to your lips. Before you sip, pause to feel the warmth and breathe it in. Then, slowly sip, using your taste buds and sense of smell to focus on the tea. What flavors are present? Can you taste flowers or herbs? If it's not too hot, hold a sip of tea in your mouth for a few seconds and truly savor the subtle flavors. Use all of your senses to enjoy your tea as though it were the first cup of tea you have ever experienced.

Meditation to Open Your Heart to the Cosmos

As you meditate, you may first find there the people, places, and things that you already care about. You may hold your family and friends in your heart, or your hometown, or some woods where you played as a child. This is a very good place to begin—indeed, where else can you begin except with the familiar? But to open your heart to the cosmos, you have to move beyond the familiar. All of these intentions should take place within your heart center. You can visualize this in the anatomically correct fashion or stylized into a Valentine's Day heart. You can picture it as a box, a room, a temple, or other concrete space. Superimpose images of the people, creatures, and things that you are reflecting on and thinking about.

1. Open up your circle to include strangers, both those nearby and those in faraway countries, especially places experiencing war or natural- or human-caused disasters. Hold in your heart prisoners of conscience and just plain prisoners and send forth the intention that they receive humane treatment and fair trials.

2. Then move to the animal kingdom and hold in your heart. Send forth your well wishes to all creatures, that they may have sufficient habitat, food, and clean water.

3. Then reflect on trees and plants, appreciating their good qualities and the way they provide for you (and for all of us). Ask (God, the gods, the universe, the cosmic forces, the Tao, the Buddha, or fill in the blank) that the forests be preserved from destruction and that all plant species flourish.

4. Finally, reflect on the earth, the stars, the planets—the entire cosmos. Be mindful of your small place within the universe and keep the intention of not overstepping your bounds.

Meditation to Ignore the Noise

If you spend a good amount of time traveling each day, you know how stressful it can be. Whether you're commuting to and from work in a train or driving your children around town, you encounter noise, traffic, and frustrated people! Sometimes blotting out the noise is a viable option. While driving, you have to keep your focus on the road ahead—these positive mantras might help you do just that.

1. You don't have to say these aloud, although you can go that route, as well. Here are a few mantras you could try:

   - May I have peace within my heart, peace with all of my relationships, and peace with all beings.
   - Nothing will distract me from delivering my children safely.
   - Love is all I need to get through my day.
   - I hear joyful noises and feel love all around me.

2. Whatever you do, make them positive mantras, as they have a way of becoming part of your reality, manifesting what you say you want. If you practice a religion, certain prayers or lines in prayers may resonate. Otherwise, spend some time creating powerful, positive mantras that you can use in trying situations—and when you're meditating.

Making Plans Meditation

Anticipation is almost as much fun as the experience. Did you know that if you visualize a future event (or past event) in detail, as if it's happening in real time, your brain will believe that it's actually happening? That means that you get to enjoy the experience twice! If you're having a rough day, taking a moment to visualize something that will happen later that you'll enjoy—such as dinner with your family, or a movie with friends, or a long-awaited vacation—can really brighten your day.

1. Begin the visualization by coming to a quiet place. Then, think about the details: Whom will you be with? Where will you be? What will you be doing?
2. Imagine the tastes and smells and textures, the sounds and sights. If you're visualizing dinner with friends, imagine their faces as they tell you about their day or tell you about what's going on in their lives.
3. Feel the good feelings—as if they are already happening—and end your visualization by stating an intention to mindfully enjoy the upcoming experience . . . before transitioning back to your daily schedule.

Easing an Overbooked Day Meditation

Every day brings with it a big to-do list. However, on those days when "too much to do" reaches an "insanely overbooked, overstressed, freaking-out" level, it's time to stop everything. That's right: Don't do anything. Stop all thoughts. Stop the mind chatter. What you need to maintain sanity is to take a breather. This mindfulness meditation will help you stop and let go so that you're ready to tackle the insanity.

1. Lie down on a yoga mat or a rug. With your legs extended, take a few falling-out breaths (inhale through your nose and "Haaaa" out your mouth).

2. Bring your knees toward your chest, and hug your knees for another few breaths.

3. Let your arms go out to the sides, and have your feet touch the mat with your knees bent. Inhale. As you exhale, bring your knees over to the right, and look to the left. Stay in this position for a few breaths. Then inhale, and exhale as you bring your knees to the other side and look in the opposite direction.

4. Think of your body as a giant kitchen sponge, and visualize yourself wringing out all of your chattering thoughts. Think about each thought as if it is a leaf, and visualize all of the leaves flowing down a stream. Once you are "wrung out," you are ready to absorb quiet and peace.

5. Twist from side to side slowly, and as you do, exhale and wring out everything. If your mind resists and you are not able to stop the mind chatter, create the intention to replace the chattering with breath. Be patient with this intention, and remain in the meditation until you feel refreshed.

Create a Calm Kitchen

Sometimes making dinner at the end of a long day is the last thing you want to do. Try this kitchen meditation to approach the task with a positive mindset.

1. As you get ready to make dinner, play music that makes you feel like singing along (or at least inspires you).

2. As you begin your work in the kitchen, spend a few minutes remembering and reconnecting with happy memories. Doing so will help calm and center you and help you feel positive about what you're doing. Think about a time that made you feel particularly good. It could be watching your grandmother make Thanksgiving dinner and helping to stir the gravy, or helping your mother or father husk corn for corn-on-the-cob, or even the time that you had a friend over and ended up laughing over the carton of eggs you dropped on the floor.

3. Hold that memory in your mind. Remember the feelings and sensations. What did it look like and smell like? Who was there with you? Take a moment to really enjoy the memory, and then release it with a smile on your face.

Chopping Vegetables Meditation

Chopping vegetables can be really relaxing and can itself be a mindful meditation. Use it when you're preparing a lot of vegetables for a stir-fry or similar meal. Instead of being annoyed by the chore, embrace it as a time to:

1. Stand side by side with all of the vegetables laid out on the counter in front of you. Line up the vegetables to chop. Make sure that you do this slowly and use all of your senses.

   - Look at the colors of the vegetables: the bright orange of the carrots, the green of broccoli, or the white onion.
   - Feel the vegetables: the texture, the softness of the silky threads of corn on the cob, the rough skin of carrots, or the bumpy eyes of a potato. When was the last time you really appreciated a vegetable?
   - As you chop an onion, enjoy the smell and how it stings your eyes after a while. Notice the great variety of herbs, and sample their different smells.
   - Taste a raw vegetable now and then as you are chopping, and really appreciate the texture and taste. Sprinkle a little sea salt onto vegetables as you chop and enjoy the salty raw vegetable.
   - Listen to the sound of the chopping and how it sounds different with each vegetable.

2. While you are cooking, listen to the sounds of simmering or sautéing, and smell the food, savoring the scent of garlic, for example.

3. Take a moment to really appreciate and give gratitude to everyone who worked so that the food is available to you. Offer gratitude to the farmers and workers who sometimes get very little wages to harvest the food, those who work in factories to produce and prepare packaged food, the store clerk who sells the food, and so on.

Eat Slowly

Eating slowly—a meditation? Yes. With the busy pace of life these days, all too often we eat on the run or shove food in before the next activity. Slow down—your body and your mind will thank you! Invite family members to try this, too, to whatever degree they are able.

1. Make a place at your table, and sit down to eat. Look at your food, pausing to breathe, noticing the smell, the textures, the colors. Even if it is a very simple and ordinary meal, you can savor the beauty and delight of it. Even a plain bowl of oatmeal is a thing of beauty when you slow down and really look at it. Consider how it was created. How amazing is it that food emerges from the ground? Food actually growing!

2. Bow your head in gratitude for the food, pick up your fork or spoon, and take a bite. Let the food linger on your tongue for a few seconds before you begin to chew.

3. Chew slowly, for a long time, and really taste each bite. You may think something is bland, and then with further investigation realize that it's actually sweet. Eat your entire meal like this, slowly and mindfully.

Sacred Reading Meditation

Find one of the classics of the world's religions and select a chapter for reading. Consider the Tao Te Ching, the Dhammapada, the Bhagavad Gita, the Ramayana, the Qur'an, the Psalms, the Gospels, or some other well-known, time-honored text.

1. Familiarize yourself with the book ahead of time and choose a chapter that "spoke" to you especially. If you underline or highlight while you read, choose a chapter that has a lot of your own personal notations. That is a good sign that there is material for you to work with.

2. As you read the text, look for a portion that speaks to you directly. A phrase will seem to jump off the page, as though it was meant specifically for you at this moment in your life. Turn the phrase over in your mind again and again until you have it memorized.

3. Then shut your eyes and allow it to continue to repeat in your mind, filtering all distractions and focusing solely on the words. You may even boil the text down to a single word or image, which can become the touchstone for gathering your attention.

4. When you have five to ten minutes left begin a quiet dialogue with yourself about the text. Ask how you can apply its insights to your life. You may find that, in a flash of inspiration, you have the answer that you have been seeking. If nothing comes to you, don't sweat it. Try again later with the same passage or a different one.

Phone Call Meditation

Whether you're a busy mom, harried career person, or enjoying retirement—we all need the support of a cherished relationship. Find a friend whom you can trust, with whom you can speak candidly and truthfully, someone who is caring and has a genuine concern for your needs and feelings and has a sense of humor. How great to be able to laugh at yourself and not take yourself too seriously. A true friend will encourage, accept, and support you, no matter what is happening in your life. We all have a need for true friendship, to receive it and to give it as well.

1. Once you have a trusted friend, you can prearrange a convenient time for a phone conversation, or occasionally call her when emotional emergencies occur.
2. Always make sure you are comfortable, maybe with your feet elevated and a cup of tea within reach before placing the call.
3. Don't use the phone call as an opportunity to vent; think of it as a meditation, a talking meditation that will help you relieve stress and feel grounded. Choose to mindfully talk with your friend, asking for her support during a stressful time, mindfully connecting with someone who understands and cares about you.

Tense and Release

If you're still wired toward the end of your day, you can try tense-and-release exercises. Begin by paying attention to your breathing. Is it fast, or slow? Close your eyes, and breathe slowly in and out, drawing your breath into your tummy and then slowly blowing out all of the air. Then, focus on each body part as described.

1. Start with your toes. Tense or curl your toes under, inhale, and then relax your toes as you exhale.
2. Tense your feet by pretending you are pointing your toes toward your forehead and pushing your heels away. Inhale while they are tense, and as you exhale, relax your feet.
3. Tense or squeeze your buttocks and your entire legs, feet, and toes at the same time. Inhale, and as you exhale, release your buttocks, legs, feet, and toes.
4. Pull your stomach in tight, until your ribcage is sticking out; bring your shoulders up to your ears. Inhale, and as you exhale, relax your tummy and your shoulders.
5. Clench your arms and your hands (making a tight fist), lifting them about 1 or 2 inches off the bed. Inhale, and as you exhale, relax your arms and hands, gently dropping them back on the bed.
6. Close your eyes really tight, and close your mouth really tight. Inhale, and as you exhale, relax your face.
7. Clench your entire body, including your buttocks and face, and inhale. Hold this for a few seconds, and then, as you exhale, say a really long "Ahhhhhhhh."

Memory Meditation

If you're having a lot of trouble unwinding, it often helps to focus on past memories, particularly ones that tap into times when you felt safe, happy, and loved.

1. Crawl in bed or sit in a comfortable chair and think about a time when you were particularly happy. Let's say it was when you rented a cottage at the beach.

2. Pause for a few breaths, giving yourself time to remember. If memories don't spring to mind for you, think about what your favorite part of the cottage was—the screened-in porch? The large picture window?

3. Close your eyes as you think back to those happy days, and try to see the cottage in your imagination: See the room where you slept, hear the sound of the waves coming to shore, remember the taste of the salty sea. Pause for a few breaths to form pictures in your mind.

4. To draw yourself deeper into the meditation, remember the weather: Was it hot and sunny? Was it cloudy? Did it rain all week? Do you remember how it smelled after the rain?

5. Slow your breathing down and whisper "Hhhoooommme" ("home") as you exhale, replicating the sound of the ocean waves as they come to shore.

6. Keep breathing slowly in and out, saying "Hhhooommme" (this is called ujjayi or ocean breath) as you exhale. Soon you will find yourself very relaxed.

Meditation for the Bath

Turn off overhead lights and light a few candles. Add a fragrant bath oil or bath salts, and play soft, soothing music, if you like.

1. Once you are in the water, take a few deep breaths and exhale with a soothing "Ahhhhhhh." Notice how light your body feels when submerged in the water.

2. Imagine the water washing away the stresses of the moment so you can emerge feeling refreshed and rested.

3. Say a prayer of gratitude for the bath and for the clean water. A prayer of gratitude can be as simple as "Thank you for the bath."

4. Use all of your senses while in the tub. Notice how the water ripples when you move your arms or legs. Focus on the ripples and the bouncing reflections of light they create.

5. Lie still until the water stills. Allow the warm water to hug your body, noticing how comfortable your body feels clothed in water.

6. Spend the next few minutes offering prayers of gratitude for the beauty of your body, for the way in which your body serves you. Begin the prayer of gratitude with your feet. Think about how your feet take you on the journey through your life, how they are able to support the rest of your body. Look down at those amazing feet, and invite your foot muscles to relax.

7. Next, consider your legs. Notice your calves, lifting one leg at a time just to watch the water run off. Notice the beautiful curve of your calves, and give thanks to your legs for the work they do for you. If you notice any critical thoughts entering, politely invite them to leave. Imagine the warm

water caressing your legs, improving circulation. Take a few deep breaths, and end by saying "Ahhhhhhh."

8. Notice your hips and belly, and offer them an extra prayer of gratitude. Draw in another deep breath, ending with "Ahhhh."

9. Notice the beautiful colors of your body, the warm skin tones, the rosy blush forming from the warmth of the water. Honor your body as a work of art.

10. Lift your arms out of the water, and look at them, noticing how the steam rises off them. Stroke your arms gently with your hands, thanking them for their strength.

11. Bring your focus to your hands, offering them a special prayer of gratitude. Your hands contain and transmit so much loving energy, and their touch offers love and healing to your family. They hold, hug, and comfort your children and others whom you love. They cook and clean and do a myriad of things that help you care for those you love.

12. Gently stroke your face with your hands. This is the face your husband and children love. Offer thanks to your face, your smile, your eyes.

13. Bring your palms together, and lower them to your chest, pressing your thumbs into your heart center in a final prayer of gratitude.

14. Before you end your bath, close your eyes, and smell the scent of the soap or oil you are using. Listen to the water as you slowly move around. After the water begins to cool, prepare to slowly surrender your bath.

15. When you are ready, wrap yourself in a thirsty towel, and slather lotion on your arms and legs and everywhere you want to retain moisture.

16. Before you slip into your pajamas, lift your arms up and over your head, gently arching your back while you enjoy a few more "Ahhhh" breaths. Enjoy the rest of the night feeling relaxed, scented, and rejuvenated.

Legs Up the Wall Meditation

Not only is putting your legs up the wall great for circulation, it will also calm you when you are agitated and stressed—perfect for an evening stress-relief session. It takes so little effort and is surprisingly relaxing.

1. Find a quiet place in your home, and bring a blanket and a pillow with you.

2. Begin by sitting up straight with your right hip against the wall.

3. Bend your knees, and swivel around until you get your legs up the wall. Your butt should be touching the wall. Your body and legs should form a right angle.

4. Once you are in position, to achieve the natural curve of your back, lift your hips and put the pillow under them, nestling it into the small of your back. You want a gentle lift of your hips, with your tailbone spilling over the pillow toward the wall. You may want to put a small folded blanket or rolled towel behind your neck to lengthen your neck and allow your chin to be at the same height as your forehead. This should feel comfortable and natural.

5. When you are settled into the pose, you can begin the meditation, bringing awareness to all of your bodies— physical, emotional, mental, and spiritual:

   • Scan your physical body, from the crown of your head to your toes. Bring your awareness to the top of your head, and notice every sensation there. Then bring awareness to your face and to all of the muscles around your eyes, jaw, neck, shoulders, and arms, all the way to your fingertips. Work your way slowly down the back and the front of your body—chest, belly, pelvic floor—always resting for a few breaths in each body part and acknowledging any feeling that may be present. Work your way down from your hips, legs, and knees to your ankles, feet, and toes. Imagine that you divide your body in half. Notice just the right side, and then notice just the left side. Take a moment to reflect on the differences you feel in each body part.

- Next, move to your emotional body. Notice any emotions that may be present. Are you anxious about the coming week? Are you still happy after meeting your friends for a quick brunch? Is there a feeling you've been reluctant to acknowledge, even to yourself? Really take the time to look at each emotion and bring awareness to it.

- Scan your mental body. Notice thoughts, images, chatter, or whatever is present at the moment. Your mental body may be very busy, even mid-meditation. Just notice what kind of chattering is going on. Are you making lists, planning, going over a past conversation, or reliving a past experience? Don't linger on any one thought too long. Just notice and be aware.

- Finally, bring awareness to your spiritual body. Does your spirit feel light or burdened? Do you feel any connection to your spirit? To a spiritual force of the universe? Don't make any judgments; just notice.

6. Use your breath and visualize letting all of this go with your exhale. Inhale and feel your breath filling your lungs, and exhale everything out. Give yourself a few minutes to continue to "watch" your breath. With every exhale, let something go. You may be letting go of a tight hip or a feeling of sadness. Once you feel that a lot has been let go, just enjoy the sensation of your breath. Stay as long as you are able.

7. When you are ready, bend your knees and roll to one side. Stay there for a few breaths, and then press yourself up and stay seated for a few breaths. When you are ready, come to a standing position, wrap your arms around yourself, and give yourself a hug.

Pray Slowly

Slowing down can bring you to a place of acceptance—acceptance of who you are and what you have, acceptance of your family, your friends, your financial situation, your community, and the world. Slowing down can become a meaningful, mindful practice.

1. Come to a comfortable cross-legged posture on a rug or yoga mat. Inhale and exhale slowly, until it feels very natural. Shake your hands rapidly, and then rest your hands on your knees, palms upward.

2. Bring all of your awareness to your fingertips. Feel the tip of each and every finger and thumb. As you think of each one, move it just slightly. You may feel almost a pulse at your fingertips or a throbbing sensation. Very slowly lift your hands off your knees, bringing them toward each other very slowly. Feel as though the space between your hands is thick. Move as slowly as you are able, as though your hands were moving themselves. Notice the tiniest detail of the movement.

3. Bring your hands together in front of your heart center, and press your thumbs into the center of your sternum. Stay for a few minutes in slowness. When you are ready, pray slowly, with true intention.

Cobbler's Pose

This pose gets its name from the position that cobblers in India traditionally assume while they work. Despite its work-related origin, it is a great relaxation pose, designed to open the hips and release tension. You can do it anytime, but it is especially effective when done in bed at the end of the day.

1. To begin, lie on your back in bed. Bend your knees, bringing your feet closer to your hips, and then open your knees to the sides. To make it more comfortable, you can put a pillow under each knee.

2. You can read a book while in this pose (make sure you have sufficient reading light) or just hold the pose for a few minutes in the dark before you fall asleep.

Sleep Meditation

It's easier to fall asleep when your body is relaxed. Naturally, this is difficult to achieve when you are worried and tense. But simple muscle-toning exercises can help. Be sure to maintain conscious breathing with a sleep meditation because good oxygenation will induce a relaxed state and encourage yawning—always a good precursor to sleep.

1. Lie on your back, hands on stomach, legs extended, eyes half closed. Avoid curling your body in a ball or lying on your side.
2. Gradually focus on your body, from the feet up. Focus your attention only on your bodywork. Starting with the feet, turn them in and curl your toes downward, as tightly as possible. As you do this, inhale. Release slowly while exhaling. Move to your calves, turn them inward and tighten the muscles while inhaling. Release slowly while exhaling. Now focus on your thighs, tightening the muscles while inhaling. Release slowly while exhaling. Move your attention to the torso. As you inhale, allow your stomach to expand fully. Slowly exhale.
3. Tense and then release your hands while inhaling and exhaling. Do the same with your arms and hands, while raising your shoulders upward toward your ears. Inhale and exhale while tensing and releasing. Tense your head by raising your chin upward as far as possible while inhaling. Slowly release it downward while exhaling. Avoid twisting your neck to the right or left.
4. Finally, perform three conscious breaths while wriggling your fingers and toes.

Dream Journal Meditation

The objective of dream meditation is to exercise attention and mindfulness in the dream state. At the same time, you are making the unconscious dimension accessible. This makes it easier to "break through" everyday thoughts and feelings while dreaming and reach the deeper stillness of meditation. Dream meditation is very simple, but it requires dedication: You will need to practice it consistently. Once you decide to pursue it, incorporate it into your daily regimen. You only need a few tools: a journal for recording your dreams and a lamp near your sleeping area. You may awaken early and want to write down a dream immediately.

1. Record your dreams on awaking. Never do it later; the details will be lost or even forgotten. Take the time to write down the dream from beginning to end. If you do not recall a dream when you wake up, open the journal and record the date with "no dream." Remember: the habit you are establishing is as important as the dream content itself.

2. Read your dream journal at your meditation oasis. If you aren't able to do this, read the journal before you retire in your sleeping area. After reading the dream, close your eyes and place yourself in the dream once more. Pay attention to the details of the environment, the people with you, the words said, and the actions performed. Open your eyes and reread the recorded dream. Are there details your meditation revealed that are not recorded? If so, add them as an "afterword."

3. After comparing what you read with what you've recalled, reflect on the meaning. You will discover unopened messages as you go through the process of recording, reading, recalling, and reflecting.

PART III

Finding Mindfulness

Understanding the Mind

The practice of meditation requires a faculty you depend on every moment of every day: your mind. Your mind can transport you to new states of being. Through meditation, you can discover the wonderful facets your mind possesses and use those functions to develop truly enhanced mental skills. But the literature of meditation, from pragmatic approaches to spiritual teachings, is loaded with references to the challenges the mind poses. One of the most difficult obstacles is that your mind can actually *obstruct* the awareness you seek. How does your mind get in the way? By too much thinking, analyzing, and worrying. To counter-balance this, you can learn techniques for controlling, relaxing, and focusing your mind.

Levels of Consciousness

Psychologists know that your mind consists of several components or levels. Learning more about them can help you understand how your mind works.

The Waking Conscious

The conscious mind is the one you are most familiar with. It is your immediate involvement with the present and it encompasses the functions of your senses. Sight, hearing, touch, taste, and scent involve your attention and evoke responses that you may or may not manage, according to your will. The waking conscious constantly brings information and challenges to your attention. Associating, recognizing, analyzing, and comparing are all functions of this level.

The waking conscious is a fundamental and necessary component of existence. No meditation practice will exclude that, so don't worry about "losing consciousness" or entering a trance or deep state of hypnosis. In fact, meditation depends on a well-developed waking conscious mind. Many meditation exercises will assist in making this possible.

The Unconscious or Subconscious

The unconscious is sometimes called the subconscious, what is below or beneath consciousness. It is a realm to which psychology and religion have given great attention, and for good reason. The unconscious stores everything that the waking conscious delegates to the back burner. The unconscious also holds memories, symbols, feelings, and thoughts that are not pertinent to your immediate needs.

An example of the power of the unconscious is the activity of dreams. The unconscious produces activity and information according to its own agenda, which certainly is your agenda but not necessarily your choice. So you are, in a sense, subject to the currents of the unconscious mind.

Meditation is a proven way to reach and understand the unconscious mind. In fact, some preliminary meditation experiences may evoke images and insights in the unconscious that are surprising or unsettling. But the more that meditation is practiced, the more familiar this territory becomes. The unconscious mind can yield solutions to pressing problems and awaken strengths we never knew we had. In addition, those "involuntary" levels, such as physiological states and emotional expressions, are found in the unconscious. It becomes possible to communicate with those levels through meditation.

The Superconscious

Different traditions view the superconscious in different ways and call it by different names, but the premise is basically the same: the intangible, spiritual nature of human existence. It is the self in Jungian psychology, the soul of Christianity, the divine body of several mystical traditions, the *atman* in Yoga philosophy, and the Buddha nature in Buddhism.

Is knowledge of the superconscious possible? According to most meditation systems, it certainly is. In fact, the goal of many schools of thought is to not only discover this dimension but integrate it with the mind and body, to achieve the full realization of our potential as human beings. The superconscious is also seen as a dimension in which we can cultivate advanced powers such as healing, hypersense, and rejuvenation. There are many examples of this potential: the physical prowess of yogis and practitioners of the martial arts, the longevity of meditation masters, and the marvelous calm and serenity achieved by those who embrace deep prayer and devoted work. Is this potential accessible by ordinary people? According to both secular and religious meditation traditions, yes; it is the inevitable result of consistent and dedicated practice.

All the traditional meditation systems agree that reaching the superconscious is a gradual process that requires constant practice. That is why meditation is called a practice, because it is a continuous process of unfolding our skill to reach beyond our ordinary state of awareness.

The Practice of Mindfulness

In its simplest terms, meditation is a quieting of the mind. It's using your breath to slow things down, relax, and connect with the *you* in you—the parts of yourself that can become blurred or overrun by the demands of daily life. Some forms of meditation are called *mindfulness meditation*. This means paying attention to your thought process, choosing to slow thoughts or to discard them, welcoming peaceful thoughts, and paying attention to what is happening right here, right now. Often, mindfulness means turning off distractions and focusing on whatever you are doing. Mindfulness can also mean choosing to do what you are doing with intention or a chosen purpose.

Many of the exercises in Part II of this book fall under the category of mindfulness meditation:

- You may get up one morning and try the Awakening Meditation, stating your intention for the day ahead.
- On another occasion, perhaps you try the Mindful Shower Meditation.
- You might focus on remaining mindful while trying the Corpse Pose (Savasana).

Exercises like these can help focus your mind in the morning, provide a much needed break midday, or help clear your mind for sleep at night.

If you are new to the concept of mindfulness, you might have found it a bit confusing or difficult to achieve. This experience is very common. In our busy, modern lives, we tend to be much more focused on what's coming up (a work deadline, dinner plans) than what's happening in the moment. Mindfulness is the art of paying attention—in the present, on purpose, without judgment. It's solely about bringing full awareness to where you are—the feelings and thoughts that are happening in your life, right here, right now. It may take some work to shift into this type of awareness, but the benefits of practicing far outweigh the challenges in achieving it.

The Benefits of Mindfulness

The practice of mindfulness can help you:

- **Learn how to stay open and choose how your mind thinks**, rather than allowing random or preconceived thoughts to control you.
- **Train your mind to focus on the more positive experiences in life.** By slowing down your habitual thought processes and directing your mind to savor small moments, you become more aware of the positive aspects in life as opposed to the negative ones.
- **Reduce stress.** When Dr. Shauna L. Shapiro, coauthor of *The Art and Science of Mindfulness*, studied the effects of mindfulness meditation on medical students, she found that the students in the meditation group were significantly less stressed than the control group and reported significantly greater levels of empathy and spirituality.
- **Process emotions.** The ongoing practice of mindfulness meditation can help you to deal with difficult emotions, as well as be less reactive and more fully present in general. It can help you feel more peaceful, more compassionate, and kinder—toward yourself and others.

Living Mindfully

Mindfulness is not confined to meditation. After developing this skill as much as possible, you carry the awareness within you. It's applied to everything you do, from eating and working to learning and relaxing. The experiences in each day, from the insignificant to the momentous, become rich and vibrant when you meet them with mindfulness. For most, it's not possible to engage mindfulness at every single moment of the day. But the practice is rewarding, and there will come a time when it becomes the way you live your life.

It's as easy as slowing down your morning routine and performing each step with intention and focus, as though every single thing you do is the most important thing you have to do in your life. If you're new to mindfulness, it helps to focus on your breath for a few minutes and use that focus to quiet your mind. Then, you gather your senses and bring your full consciousness to what you are doing. Physically slow down, paying attention to sensory input (such as the feel of your clothing as it glides over your skin, or the sound of the water running when you brush your teeth). If your mind wanders, always go back to focusing on your breath. This may feel awkward at first, but what you want to avoid is habitually (and unconsciously) rushing through these activities.

As you are brushing your teeth, for example, try not to think of the next activity. Instead, bring all of your attention to what's happening in that moment: the feel of the brush as you use it to massage your gums and clean your teeth, the way your mouth feels sparkling clean after you rinse. Isn't it great that you have teeth to brush? Smile at yourself in the mirror!

Mindfulness is about staying focused on what's happening right here, right now, avoiding thoughts of the past or the future. In the preceding example, just breathing and brushing . . . breathing and brushing. It's also about savoring experiences and feeling gratitude for your blessings.

Mastering Self-Acceptance

Self-acceptance is one of the goals of mindfulness meditation. When you observe the thoughts that pass through your mind, you should observe your reactions to them as well. What you may not expect is the criticism you often level at yourself—blaming yourself, for example, for thinking "wrong" versus "right" thoughts about yourself or others, or for your actions or lack thereof in recalled situations. These patterns of thinking come from conditioning and past experience, and they are of no use in growing and understanding. Not judging yourself is difficult enough. But when the criticism and high expectations diminish, you need to nourish yourself. Meditation is a way of addressing that, but insights may come simply from opening your heart to the fullness of life you seek.

Meditation Is Action

Though it may not seem like it at first, meditation is a form of action, not an escape or a distraction. Meditation hones the razor-sharp focus that you need to do things well, and the attitude and insight you need to ignore false beliefs and emotions. Meditation allows you to see when you have encountered a genuine problem, and when you're dealing with a drama created by your ego. It helps you cut through the addiction to extrinsic reward and find satisfaction in the present moment. It also helps you stop worrying.

Meditation will not magically carry the day for you, but it will help you to work at your best, channeling all of your energies into a single objective. Peppering your day with meditation breaks leads to fewer distractions, because meditation sharpens the mind and gives it the ability to decompress and fine-tune itself.

Single-Pointed Awareness

No matter where you are in life, your purpose in meditation is to maintain *single-pointed awareness*—staying completely immersed in the present moment. All memories of the past and desires for the future vanish, and the present takes on a new fullness as you remain with it in meditation.

You can accomplish this in the following way:

1. Engaging in only one thing at a time externally . . .
2. While entertaining only a single point of awareness internally.

While meditating, this means only focusing on your breathing or your visualization. When you're not formally meditating, this means concentrating solely on the task at hand and giving it your full presence of mind and body.

Creating Gray Space

What does it mean to create *gray space*? One of the best ways to understand it is to think about childhood. When you were young, you could sit and watch the pattern of raindrops as they cascaded down a car window, or observe the pattern of lichen on a stone. You could lie in bed on a Saturday morning and talk to yourself for hours, or take a handful of sand and let it flow through your fingers. These in-between moments are not exactly meditation and are not exactly intentional actions either. It's this type of gentle activity that is most vulnerable to being edited out of our heavily scheduled adult lives.

Unwasting Your Wasted Time

When you live mindfully and incorporate meditation into your days, you will notice that you have downtime, when you don't have anything that you are *supposed* to be doing. You will realize for the first time just how much of your time was wasted before. After putting the material in this book into practice, you will begin to have empty spaces in your life. Avoid the temptation to convert these gains into more frenetic activity, or you will find yourself right back where you started. Use at least half of this time to do nothing at all—not even meditate.

Create gray spaces that are not meditating, not daydreaming, not really anything. Allow yourself to go into a kind of mental hibernation. Your mind needs this downtime in order to recuperate, and it is doing a lot of work behind the scenes when you least expect it. With any remaining time after meditating and doing nothing, work on those neglected priorities that you have been putting on the back burner.

Meditation for Memory and Creativity

Throughout this book you've read about the myriad benefits of meditation on the body, but what about the mind? Though these effects may be less tangible than lower blood pressure or a decreased cholesterol count, they can still have an enormous impact in various areas of your life. Two major examples of this are found in the areas of memory and creativity. Meditation can help you preserve and enhance your memory by helping you access where memories are stored. Meditation can also improve your creativity and help you overcome blocks.

Meditation and Memory

Memory loss can be caused by dozens of factors, ranging from the aftereffects of surgery or medication, to diseases like Alzheimer's and Parkinson's, to alcohol and drug abuse, to mental health concerns like anxiety and depression. Each cause has its own particular origin and treatment program, including necessary medical and psychological interventions, but meditation can improve the situation for you no matter the cause.

When it comes to preserving good memory, what is good for the heart is also good for the brain. The same diet that controls blood pressure and cholesterol also supports the health of your brain; in the same way, meditative techniques that slow your heart rate and lower blood pressure also lead to better brain functioning.

Studies have shown that meditation reduces the risk of memory loss, stroke, and other disorders in old age, and also improves memory for those already over age sixty. According to a study by Sanford I. Nidich in the *Journal of Social Behavior and Personality*, the benefits cut across a wide range of mental factors, inducing higher levels of nonverbal and verbal intelligence, long-term memory, and speed of processing.

Meditation not only improves memory in the elderly; it also helps students to perform well on standardized tests, executives to achieve job results, and parents to remember to pick up the dry cleaning and the kids from soccer practice.

Why does meditation improve memory? The medical explanations are complex and not fully understood, but part of the reason lies in our typical inattention as we go about our daily lives. Most of the time, it's not so much that our memories are faulty but that a memory never got formed in the first place. If you have ever lost your keys, this may be all too familiar. You set them down without paying attention to what you are doing, so your brain has no mental picture to recall when the time comes to find them again.

Meditation and Creativity

People often think of creativity as an innate quality, something you either have or you don't. But people who think they are not creative simply may not be in the habit of being creative. And many people tend to judge their own efforts too harshly. This self-deprecating attitude leaves very little room for experimentation, which is a vital part of the creative process.

Expanding creative ability requires wiggle room, space that comes from leaving well enough alone, nonjudgment, and repeated attempts. Without safe space and time, creativity simply can't get off the ground. Meditation can help you to refrain from judgment and to stop listening to the internal critic, who is never satisfied.

At the other extreme are people who think they are geniuses, that everything they do is simply perfect. This attitude, too, stifles creativity because it prevents further growth. If you think everything you do is already perfect, you have little reason to learn something new.

How Does Meditation Stimulate Creativity?

The meditative processes described in this book grease the wheels of creativity. Meditation strengthens the architecture of your brain. You will be able to think faster, visualize better, and work more steadily. Meditation also tames the voice of the internal critic. The practice of watching thoughts will translate directly into being able to suspend the voice of judgment, especially in that fragile, early stage of creativity. Meditation taps into the intuitive layers of the self, which will create more profound expressions without conscious effort. Meditation creates intrinsic rewards, making work without validation easier to handle. You will become more self-confident, which will allow you to weather early faltering and criticism.

Meditation and creativity also complement one another by making the creative life more bearable. The histories of music, painting, and literature are rife with the stories of broken people who succumbed to mental illness and substance abuse. These tragic lives suggest that creative endeavors are not the breathless, carefree pursuits that outsiders tend to see. Oftentimes, creatives are under more pressure than people with more conventional lifestyles, because the competition for work is more fierce. Strategies for stress relief should be a part of the standard training for every artist. Meditation can bring more balance to the lives of part-time and full-time artists of all persuasions and disciplines. Meditation also reduces burnout in careers characterized by ups and downs—heights of elation and depths of despair.

Accepting Criticism

Criticism, too, has a role to play during the creative journey, because it helps sharpen skills, leading to better results. If free expression is the entrée into the creative process, taking criticism is the next threshold that must be crossed. People who can say "yes" to constructive criticism are destined to become better artists, whether or not they realize it themselves. Meditation helps in this area because it de-centers the ego and allows you to think of art as happening through you but not necessarily by you. The meditative artist views herself as a channel for energies coming from outside the self, while the egotistical artist views art as something coming *de novo*, from her own genius.

Creativity for Its Own Value

Another common problem that stifles creativity is the belief that creative work only "counts" if it reaches a mass audience. Emily Dickinson stashed her poems in baskets and drawers around her house; Melville's *Moby Dick* was considered a flop when it was first published. Would anyone consider these writers as lacking in creativity?

What reaches a mass audience today may be considered rubbish one hundred years from now, and what is obscure today may become a cultural mainstay in another generation. In fact, every new trend begins on the margins of society before the marketing machines get ahold of it. So creatives must have the courage to explore and do something new; otherwise, nothing new ever gets made.

Active Mind versus Receptive Mind

Have you ever tried to untangle an electrical cord? If you just keep pulling it toward you, the knots only get worse and the tangles won't come undone. It's tempting to do this when you're frustrated, but it's counterproductive. Sometimes, if you pull in the opposite direction, loosening the knots, you can more easily see how to untangle the cord.

It's like that with your mind too, which has more than one direction in which it can go. Your thoughts have an active direction and a receptive direction. We spend most of our time in the active direction: The active mind solves a sudoku, thinks of the right word, makes a grocery list, and does anything that requires conscious thought. The receptive mind listens for a faint sound, takes in a painting, and feels the breeze.

Keep in mind: there's a difference between *receptivity* and *passivity*. To be receptive is not to be passive. Meditation is not tuning out or escaping to another world or even clearing your mind; it is setting aside anything that interferes with your complete engagement with reality. It would be more correct to call it *an escape from escapism*.

Still other activities have active *and* receptive dimensions. An amateur golfer plays only with the active mind, while a pro golfer blends the active and the receptive. The same can be said for gardening, skiing, or almost any other physical activity.

The person who thinks only with the active part of the mind will have difficulty responding to changing conditions and will be easily frustrated. The person who can listen and respond will be calmer and, paradoxically, more in control of the situation than the person who plans and attacks.

Meditation is about training the mind to emphasize the receptive dimension, relearning a capacity for listening, for wonder and awe. Meditation teaches us to set aside our own agendas and encounter the world. This can be difficult, because it feels like a loss of control, like giving up something, like taking a risk. It is indeed all of these things. But in return, we gain more vivid experiences and flashes of real inspiration.

Balancing Your Two Minds

Fortunately, you don't have to choose between the active and the receptive. The two go together like horse and rider, and every action on our part is simultaneously a conscious exertion and an unconscious adjustment to the surroundings.

The active and the receptive are both important parts of life. Meditation just brings them into greater alignment. This means having some periods where you purposely accentuate the receptive aspect, to make the balance come closer to 50/50. This will not come naturally, because we live in an age where action rules. Quiet time goes against the grain. If you have to sit on your hands to keep from reaching for the mouse or the remote control, that's okay.

Seeing Clearly Through Meditation

In meditation, you should aim to set aside all fantasies about how the world might be, how you yourself might be, and focus on what *is*. You want to see things with their blemishes and all, without judgment or comment. Your thoughts color and obscure the world, and meditation seeks to unveil the world as it really is.

Use Meditation to Quiet the World Around You

As you begin your meditation practice, you may find that some people get defensive when they hear about it. They will say things like, "Oh, I have a short attention span; I could never focus like that" or, "I could never sit still for that long." Of course, these same people can sit and watch a feature-length film with no problem or surf the Internet for hours on end. The real problem is not a short attention span; it's how your attention is directed and to what end.

If you're accustomed to activity and passivity, the idea of receptivity—the basis of meditation—can be uncomfortable. We notice the big, flashy things rather than the small, quiet things. Our senses are burned out by the barrage of images and sounds. The mental shell-shock of living in a consumer society means we have a hard time dealing with real space and time.

Becoming Introspective

Meditation isn't just about fixing a problem or coping with the frenetic pace of society. It is an alternative way of approaching the world—a different operating system, if you will. It allows for tremendous leaps of creativity, opening doors of possibility you previously thought impossible. As you begin to explore your own mind through quiet observations, you will see how many of your limitations are self-imposed, how many of the givens of life are actually self-created. You will see just how malleable your own self-concept can be. That will give you the freedom to explore the hidden aspects of yourself. You may suddenly find that you want to throw away your entire wardrobe or listen to salsa music or move to a new town.

You may also see things about yourself that you don't like. You may notice that you have a tendency to make jokes at others' expense, or that you can be overly glum and pessimistic. These habits are deeply ingrained and will not go away overnight, but, as you notice them again and again, you can begin to change course. Just as a ship responds to the direction of its rudder, your outward habits will begin to change as you change your patterns of thinking. As you become aware of your negative character traits, you may feel guilt or self-hatred. Just let these feelings come and go, as you would any other thought that arises as you meditate.

Transformation Through Meditation

You should now see the general outlines of what happens during meditation:

- Feeling a greater acceptance for the way things are, and letting go of the need to control people and situations.
- Awakening deep intuition and creativity rather than focusing exclusively on rational thought.
- Exploring your previously censored self.
- Cultivating deep listening rather than operating based on a preconceived agenda.
- Becoming one with your surroundings.
- Discovering and eliminating self-imposed limitations and opening yourself to boundless possibility.
- Diffusing negative character traits through self-observation and course correction.

This brief list gives a rough outline of the transformation that meditation can accomplish. You don't have to be an adept who practices for years on end. Anyone can realize this transformation. The results of meditation are not some far-off place that must be reached through strenuous effort. All of these goals are achievable in the here and now of daily practice.

Meditation As a Retreat

Occasionally nothing seems to go right: Your holiday bonus has been canceled, bill collectors are calling, your boss criticizes your work, or your best friend is diagnosed with a scary disease. Suddenly you feel deflated and defeated. You want a stiff drink, a new job, or both. Where can you go when every part of life seems to be going haywire? Only one place: within.

Get Back to Basics

At times like these, forgo the visualization or chanting. Just sit. Feel the pain and anguish without having to do anything about it. You don't have to fix things, you don't have to blame yourself, and you don't have to ask "why?" Simply be present—or try to be present—for whatever is there in that moment.

The world can be a disappointing place, even for those who do their best to be compassionate and good. And at those times of crisis, the last thing that you want is someone telling you that it's all your fault. Often you are harder on yourself than anyone else would be, and meditation can help you to forgive yourself and move forward. It can help you move beyond the often stilted analysis that you make of situations and accept them without comment.

Take Refuge During Difficult Times

Meditation doesn't require faith in the innate goodness of human beings, or belief that the world is more good than bad, or that there's a God. For this reason, meditation as a practice appeals to all kinds of people at all stages of life.

If you've ever had a migraine headache, you know that the best thing to relieve it is a dark, quiet room. It doesn't take the pain away, but it makes it easier to wait it out. The refuge helps you to separate yourself from the pain, to observe it as though it does not belong to you. And the same can be said of meditation. Your inner self can be that dark room in painful times, a portable place of retreat that you always have with you. You won't be able to make problems go away by sheer force of will, but you can stop identifying with them. In this way they become less solid and real, as though you were watching them in a movie.

Find Peace

If you always try to make sense of things, you sometimes make them worse. When you stop trying to solve everything, you can find peace. *Peace* is not a matter of rainbows, unicorns, and cute puppies, or some sort of sentimental or naïve way of looking at the world. Rather, it's a matter of divesting yourself of harmful thoughts and feelings, a subtracting process of peeling away the layers of mental accretions. You peel away the good and bad thoughts and emotions, because you have stopped trusting in your own capacity to discriminate between good and bad. Even destructive tendencies present themselves to the ego as good, so oftentimes the internal feedback can be misleading. Only with a lot of experience can you read between the lines of your own propaganda.

Surrender

A kind of surrender takes place in meditation. You realize your own mortality and vulnerability, your own powerlessness. In difficult times, you can convert sorrow into sweet sorrow, the kind that reminds you that you are still alive. It may be scant consolation, but it may also keep you from deeper distress or despair. All too often we magnify our bad situations by dwelling on them. Meditation gives us ease because it helps us let go of those situations.

During the rough spots, sometimes the best thing you can do is take a step back and try to calm your frayed nerves. Meditation can be the quiet refuge that makes an untenable situation bearable. It can change the emotional filter through which you view the world, making the burden seem lighter. When you stub your toe first thing in the morning and then spill your coffee, everything seems irritating for the rest of the morning. The traffic lights seem to conspire against you, file folders rebel against your clumsy fingers, and the sound of a ringing phone makes you want to scream.

This frustrated, persecuted feeling surely has no roots in reality itself, but is formed by a mental process in which the world becomes negatively shaded. By contrast, when you deliberately cultivate peace and compassion, traffic on the way to work seems to flow better, that annoying colleague just seems amusing, not psychotic, and the leftovers you brought for lunch are the best thing you have ever eaten. This is not the wild optimism of intention manifestation or wish fulfillment or magical thinking; it is just the simple observation that our mental state changes the way that we see the world. Gently adjusting your mental state can give you the strength that you need to keep going, which might be just enough to help find a solution.

Making Time for Meditation

Finding time requires more than just good intentions. It's one thing to intend to do something or say that you value a particular activity, and another thing altogether to assign it a space on your daily agenda.

Scheduling meditation may seem a little unromantic, a little type-A, a little anal-retentive. But scheduling something means that it's important. Writing something down, especially writing by hand on a sheet of paper, has a powerful effect on the memory. By writing a schedule for your meditation, you commit to that appointment. You also say to yourself that you value your own well-being enough to take time during the day for yourself.

In the yogic tradition, the first two hours before dawn and the first two hours after sunset are considered the most auspicious times to meditate. This has to do with astrology, but it also makes sense from a practical standpoint. Before dawn, you haven't had the chance yet to get too immersed in the activities of the day, so you don't yet have to tear yourself away from them. After sunset, you have accomplished enough to call it quits and should similarly have little to bother and distract. Any later or earlier than these two time periods, and you are likely asleep or at least sleepy. So use these two windows if you can: not each whole two-hour bracket, but somewhere within those periods, find a few minutes.

What about other times during the day? How do you know when it's a good time to meditate? If you wait for a perfect time, it will never come. You will always have other things to do, and you might not always feel particularly inspired to meditate. In order for it to be effective, meditation has to be an appointment that you keep and not something you do when you feel like it. And yet, at some points during the day you would benefit more from working than from meditating because you are clearing items from the mental landscape that would interrupt your peace of mind. And there is the usual business of life: meetings, reports, classes, and the like, which do not qualify as distractions and cannot always be negotiated. So you have to be flexible and work around busy times.

Look for Small Holes in Your Schedule

Sure, you're busy. But the average day is not a solid wall of activity—it's more like Swiss cheese. The key to finding a little bit of personal time is to look for the small pockets of air. Remember, we're talking about only a few minutes at a time. Most people don't have the luxury of big two-to-four-hour blocks of time, but nearly everyone can find five-to-twenty-minute blocks.

When you identify them in your own life, schedule and commit to them in writing. When you come to the appointed time, drop everything and get settled for meditation. Be aware that something will happen that might tempt you to deviate from the plan: you will get a phone call from a client, a deadline will be changed, your e-mail will ping repeatedly. Discriminate between the true emergencies that need your attention and the routine miasma of noise that should be avoided.

Maybe you have some trouble distinguishing between emergencies and noise. Ask yourself, "Can this wait for a few minutes? Will my reputation be affected if I don't attend to this right this minute?" Tell yourself that you can get right back to whatever issue arises as soon as the meditation is over. You may even have a better handle on the issue after meditation than you did before.

If you're still having trouble letting go, meditate anyway. It is better to meditate while distracted than not to meditate at all. If you miss a session because you just can't drop what you are doing, no worries: Just get yourself back on track at the next appointed time.

Don't feel the need to atone for a missed session by adding the time to a future session: Guilt-tripping is not productive. This is about your own unfolding development and not about some imaginary yardstick of perfection. If you miss a session, it just means that this is where you are at this moment in your journey. So don't cry over lost time or a difficult season. If you have discovered meditation as part of the purpose for your life and not just an adjunct, you are not in danger of losing it entirely. You will come back to it at a later time when the life atmosphere is more conducive.

Maximize Your Free Moments

The ancient Greeks distinguished between *chronos* and *kairos*—time as it is measured in days and time as it is measured in experience. *Chronos* flows in a linear, regular fashion, while *kairos* has connotations of the appropriate or fortuitous hour. When you manage *chronos* effectively, *kairos* will toss a few freebies your way. The big meeting will be canceled, the server will go down, or the boss will catch the flu. Without taking advantage of these gifts of time deceptively, you can use them for meditation and boost your productivity.

Consciously take control of your time and see this free hour as the gift that it is. Maybe this extra time could be used to push yourself a little further than you would ordinarily go in your practice, or maybe you could read an article or book chapter that would improve your technique. Perhaps you could go outside for a walk or look into a weekend retreat.

One reason people don't feel more rested is because they fill in the breaks with more information and more noise. Your brain may not process a blog post all that much differently from a report for work. It might be marginally better if you derive happiness from it, but you are still using visual processing, language centers, and other parts of the brain. If you are trying to write the report and work on the blog post at the same time, you are definitely adding stress to your life. In order for the brain to truly rest, you have to ratchet down the level of activity. Meditation provides a real rest for the brain because it brings it down to a baseline state while simultaneously calming respiration and circulation.

Putting a meditation break into your routine is like putting a period at the end of a sentence. It lets you wind down from what came before in order to prepare for what is coming next. Running on full throttle all the time creates confusion and stress.

Seeking Out Meditation Communities

Some of the great meditation schools—spiritual, contemplative, and devotional—offer meditation training. Some offer short retreats, a few days away from the outside world, which are useful for the busy person. Other schools offer extended training periods, perhaps for a month or more, to develop specific meditation techniques. Students who attend these courses may receive certification or initiation in the discipline. Although you may not intend to teach meditation technique in the near future, training events are a way to acquire a comprehensive view. As you put the information into practice, you will appreciate the depth of experience that you acquire at longer sessions.

Retreats are another opportunity to experience meditation under the guidance of one or more leaders. A single retreat can advance your practice better than several months of practice in everyday life. Organized retreats surround you with all the components of meditation, even if you have been unable to establish them in your regular life. Quiet time, peaceful surroundings, well-selected music and readings, and people of like mind create the experience.

Ashrams and monasteries often open their facilities to part-time residents. Preparing the community's food, caring for the living quarters, and completing tasks in the library or school are activities that are expected of the student in addition to worshipping, studying, and meditating. The retreat attendant becomes part of the discipline of the community, and leaves a different person than the one who entered. If you are looking for a place to take a retreat, do an Internet search for "monastery," "ashram," or "retreat" along with the name of the desired state or region. You should be able to find a facility nearby. If this doesn't work, consider going on a solitary retreat in a park or national forest.

Working with a Teacher

Certain cultural beliefs are woven into the great meditation traditions. A novice meditator must understand these beliefs before making a commitment to enter a training program as a student or disciple with a teacher or master. In Eastern countries, centuries of tradition are incorporated in the custom of discipleship. The teacher accepts the student and imparts the sum of his or her knowledge to that pupil. This process often takes many years and requires a complete commitment in time and loyalty.

In many cases, more than study is required. The novice may tend to the teacher's needs by running errands, cooking, and cleaning the learning environment. These duties are considered a privilege for the student, and giving them to the student is a profound responsibility for the teacher. In this system, much is taught that does not involve book learning or memorizing. The student learns practical lessons through everyday experience, such as tending a garden or brewing a pot of tea.

The advantage is that the student earns the right to the teacher's exclusive knowledge and talents, and that extends into the future when the student becomes a teacher in his own right. And for the teacher, passing on personal and accumulated talents is the fulfillment of a life's work. However, a pupil is limited by the knowledge and experience of the teacher. So if you choose to study meditation with one teacher, you must have some idea of what you want and what the teacher can offer.

Realistically, specialized training in any self-improvement program is going to require a financial investment. Here are some reasonable expenses that should be covered by students:

- Rent for a reserved space in a room, school, or center
- Overhead costs, such as janitorial service and utilities
- The teacher's time (salary)
- Costs of printed materials, books, and audio or video materials
- Transportation costs for the teacher

If you are asked to donate an unspecified amount to cover your meditation program, take these expenses into account and pay accordingly. Some teachers are very dedicated and live solely on the income they obtain from their students.

Question any requests for specified amounts of money that will be applied to unspecified expenses. For example, a $100 request for the "building fund" should be voluntary and tax-deductible.

Finding the Right Community for You

Learning meditation with groups or communities can be a rewarding experience, but consider the following points when you are making the choice:

- Know exactly what the course of study or activity will entail. A program outline should be available, and it should clearly explain what will be presented and when.
- Be fully informed of the costs and responsibilities. All fees should be listed, and extras should be explained (such as "private room").
- If certain duties are required, you should be informed before you arrive. You do not want to be surprised with new or unfamiliar duties while you are there.
- Understand your living arrangements. If you are to share space with roommates, you must know that selection will be made based on your criteria and not someone else's. Likewise, sharing a bathroom or kitchen with a group of people may have other considerations, so be prepared.
- Be clear about rules and regulations. Talking, exercising, or chewing gum may be okay or strictly forbidden. Don't be shy about asking, either; you may be called on later to advise someone who is more in the dark than you are.
- Always ask what is customary for clothing and diet. You do not want to be self-conscious when everyone is wearing a kimono and you are in sweatpants.

In the final analysis, it's not necessary to look for an expert to guide you when you are starting a meditation practice. There are a number of basic steps you can take on your own to start and develop the habit of meditation. Ultimately, the process begins and ends with you.

Teaching Others

Whether you have studied some of the great traditions, have had some experience with life in a meditation community, or have done neither, you are never truly a "beginner." Everyone has some experience in meditation, either through deliberate effort or circumstance. But if you become seriously interested in teaching meditation to others, progressive training or mentorship is the best way to prepare for the work. Such training should include assisting the teacher with other students, developing your own style, and mastering as many techniques of the "school" as possible.

You should also be familiar with some terminology you'll hear along the way, including the following terms, all of which are Sanskrit, though many are used interchangeably in Yoga and in Buddhist organizations:

- **Ashram ("effort"):** In Hinduism, a group that follows or studies a particular spiritual discipline. A guru or teacher guides the disciples or students. The ashram is usually removed from everyday life and is modeled after an ascetic, simple existence.
- **Sangha ("crowd"):** In Buddhism, the group of practitioners who follow a teacher. In particular, Sangha refers to the body of teachers and followers who form the Buddhist community. The Sangha is not attached to any specific place.
- **Satsang ("good company"):** This term refers to a gathering of mutually supportive students or seekers of wisdom; it's a Yoga community that is not attached to a particular ashram.

Moving Forward

You have now begun a practice that you can continue for the rest of your life. You will have a hidden refuge of deep calm available to you any time you need it. You will find aspects of yourself you never knew were there, unlock hidden talents, and find deep intuition. You will come closer to the mystery at the heart of the universe and discover deeper connections with others. You will foster improved mental and physical health and have greater memory and creativity. The practice of meditation can be just the sort of boost you need to bring you greater satisfaction in life.

Where you go from here is up to you. You can continue with the practices in this book indefinitely; they are open-ended enough to yield benefits at all levels of practice. You may stumble onto a new spiritual tradition or return to the tradition of your childhood. Or, you may see meditation in an entirely secular light, as a way to enhance performance. No matter where this path leads, walk it in confidence, knowing that millions have gone before you.

Eventually, you may find yourself to be the leader in any room where you are present. Others will notice your calm in the face of difficult situations, and they will begin to look up to you. People will wonder where you gained such great composure. Use your abilities for good: to help other people, to advance worthwhile causes, and to look out for those at the bottom of organizational hierarchies. You will be able to see things that others can't: the subtle aspects of a situation available to someone who truly pays attention. When everyone else is afraid and confused, you will be a noticeable presence, a refuge of strength in difficult times.

If one commodity is in short supply these days, it is careful attention. The more complicated our lives become, the less we can attend to any part of life with the consideration needed. You meditate not only for yourself, but for the world. When you refuse to live an insane life, when you live with simple wisdom gained from within, you make the impossible possible. You empower others to also live productive, peaceful lives. You help to reverse the ever-present culture of fear and anxiety. In short, you become peace and love for the world.

That may sound like a lofty goal, but it is attainable for you. Just think of the strides that you have made while reading this book. The days ahead hold greater possibility than you have previously imagined, and you yourself hold more potential than ever before. Awaken to that potential, and you will change the world. Go away from these pages knowing that you hold the keys to your own destiny, that your own heart is the heart of the universe.

Suggested Reading

Dillard-Wright, David and Ravinder Jerath. *The Everything® Guide to Meditation and Healthy Living.* Avon, MA: Adams Media, 2010.

Farhi, Donna. *The Breathing Book: Good Health and Vitality Through Essential Breath Work* (New York: Owl Books, 1996).

Goldstein, Joseph and Kornfield, Jack. *Seeking the Heart of Wisdom: The Path of Insight Meditation* (Boston: Shambhala Publications, 1987).

Ihnatko, Andy. "Multitasking Is a Lie—Your Brain Needs a Break." *Chicago Sun-Times.* September 25, 2010.

Khalsa, Dharma Singh, and Cameron Stauth. *Meditation As Medicine* (New York: Fireside, 2001).

Kornfield, Jack. *After the Ecstasy, the Laundry: How the Heart Grows Wise on the Spiritual Path* (New York: Bantam Books, 2000).

Medina, John. *Brain Rules: 12 Principles for Surviving and Thriving at Work, Home, and School* (Seattle: Pear Press, 2008).

Nidich, Sanford I., et al. "Effect of the Transcendental Meditation Program on Intellectual Development in Community-Dwelling Older Adults." *Journal of Social Behavior and Personality* 17, no. 1 (2005): 217–226.

Ornstein, Robert. *The Right Mind: Making Sense of the Hemispheres* (New York: Harcourt Brace & Co., 1997).

Rahula, Walpola. *What the Buddha Taught* (New York: Grove Press, 1974).

Trungpa, Chögyam. *Training the Mind and Cultivating Loving-Kindness* (Boston: Shambhala Publications, 1993).

Walker, Evan Harris. *The Physics of Consciousness: The Quantum Mind and the Meaning of Life* (Cambridge, MA: Perseus Books Group, 2000).

Index